the **complete** *series*

Gluten-free

& multi-allergy cookbook

Lola Workman

WILEY

John Wiley & Sons, Inc.

Published by John Wiley & Sons, Inc., Hoboken, New Jersey

For general information on our other products and services or for technical support, please
contact our Customer Care Department within the United States at (800) 762-2974, outside
the United States at (317) 572-3993 or fax (317) 572-4002.

Wiley also publishes its books in a variety of electronic formats. Some content that appears
in print may not be available in electronic books. For more information about Wiley
products, visit our web site at www.wiley.com.

Library of Congress Cataloging-in-Publication Data is available upon request.

ISBN 978-1-118-11976-1

Printed in China

10 9 8 7 6 5 4 3 2 1

Contents

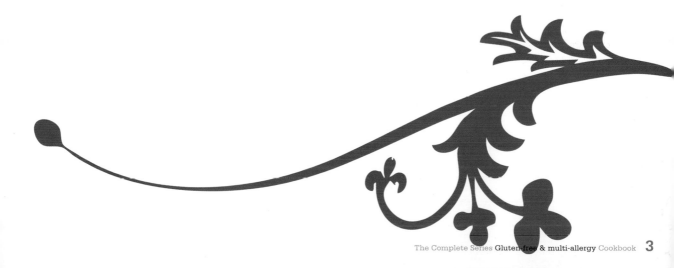

Introduction

The first step with cooking with dietary restrictions is to recognize and memorize the list of foods that are allowed in your diet. Your dietician or doctor can provide a list of the foods you must avoid and this book will help you select ingredients to replace those foods.

Once you have this information, you'll be accustomed to reading the labels of every product that you buy. Buying a pre-mixed product, such as gluten-free flour is not always a good idea if it doesn't list the specific ingredients. Some gluten-free products can still contain milk products or other chemicals or ingredients that you cannot tolerate.

Using these recipes will help you plan your nutritionally balanced diet that is also satisfying. If you have never made breads and desserts, don't worry. Some of the methods for gluten-free cooking are different from traditional baking, so follow the step by step instructions carefully.

Remember that fresh baked bread is made to be eaten the day it's made, just like it was centuries ago. Commercial ingredients to extend the shelf life of bread products often contain gluten, so you'll need to avoid them. Once you get organized, you'll soon learn that baking homemade breads is incredibly fulfilling.

Pre-mixes can be weighed in exact quantities, then bagged and kept in your cupboard until you are ready to bake. When you are blending your own flour, always mix at least 6 pounds at a time and store it in a large cotton bag so it will keep indefinitely. Our test kitchens have used this method and flour that was stored for 4 years this way, was still fresh and ready to use.

Nutritional Value of Ingredients

Amaranth flour – Extremely high in nutritional value, amaranth flour is higher in protein than most commonly used grains, with the exception of quinoa. It has a near perfect balance of amino acids, and is very high in fiber, iron, manganese, phosphorus and magnesium. It also has a high content of calcium, pantothenic acid, potassium, protein, vitamin B6 and zinc. Unlike most grains, amaranth is high in vitamin C and also contains vitamin A.

Fine rice flour – Rice originated in Asia but is now grown in many different parts of the world. It differs from most other cereals as it needs to be planted on land that is submerged with water, though some varieties do grow in upland areas.

Rice is a good source of carbohydrates, but doesn't have quite as much protein as some other cereals. Rice flour, because of the lack of gluten, cannot be used to make a yeasted loaf, but can be used for cakes, biscuits and pancakes. Rice flakes, both brown and white, can be added to muesli or made into a milk pudding or porridge.

Tapioca starch – Milled from the dried starch of the cassava root (a woody perennial shrub native to Brazil and Paraguay, now widely grown in the tropics and subtropics) tapioca starch is recovered by wet-grinding the washed roots and continuous re-washing – resulting in a pure carbohydrate. The starch grains, once released from the strained pulp, are dried to a paste then milled into flour. The unmodified starch is called native tapioca starch or native tapioca flour and is a fine white powder. Best used in combination with other flours, it is gluten-free and easy to digest.

Potato flour and starch – Although tapioca starch is often used to replace arrowroot in recipes, they are slightly different, but as they are both clear starches they are usually interchangeable.

Potatoes are dried and then ground to a powder to make this flour, which is high in carbohydrates. It is also a good source of vitamin B6, iron, zinc, niacin, potassium, manganese, magnesium, phosphorus, thiamine, vitamin C and fiber.

Garbanzo bean flour – Garbanzo bean flour is called dhal flour or channa dahl in India, while in England and most of Europe it is known as gram flour. The highest quality flour comes from India and is golden in color with no brown specs of skin.

Made from roasted chickpeas, which are very high in protein, this flour is a wonderful source of fiber and contains most vitamins and minerals. It also contains lots of fabulous antioxidants. Chickpeas are high in complex carbohydrates, meaning they provide energy over a long period, making them a great help for diabetics as they produce little demand on insulin.

Blending Your Own Flour

Formulation of these recipes came as a result of my cooking classes for food intolerance for those who cannot tolerate wheat or gluten in their diets. I have avoided using soy flour as many people are intolerant to it and children particularly don't like the strong taste.

Nutrition should be considered when you are selecting a gluten-free replacement for wheat flour as simple mixes of rice and cornstarch do not provide enough nutrition to replace wheat, particularly for children.

My bread and pastry flour can be used in all recipes to replace all-purpose flour – important if you are intolerant to corn or salicylates. This flour is lighter and drier so if you are using it for cakes, 1 tablespoon of almond meal or other nut meal to each 100g of flour will increase the moisture level.

Although all recipes in this book were thoroughly tested using the superfine flour blend, any of these blends can be used in most of the recipes in this book. Some will give a better result than others, depending on the recipe, but they can all be used for both my sauce blocks and for cookies and pastry. Select the blend that suits your dietary requirements and continue using this blend throughout.

Lola's All-Purpose Flour

400g/14 oz garbanzo bean flour
400g/14 oz maize cornstarch
200g/7 oz potato flour
200g/7 oz corn flour

Lola's Bread and Pastry Flour

400g/14 oz garbanzo bean flour
400g/14 oz potato flour
200g/7 oz fine rice flour
200g/7 oz arrowroot

Superfine Flour

200g/7 oz garbanzo bean flour
200g/7 oz potato starch
150g/5 oz tapioca starch
100g/3¼ oz fine rice flour

Grain-Free Blend

200g/7 oz garbanzo bean flour
200g/7 oz tapioca starch
100g/3½ oz potato starch
100g/3½ oz buckwheat flour or amaranth flour

Potato-Free Blend

200g/7 oz white sorghum flour
200g/7 oz fine white rice flour
100g/3½ oz brown rice flour
100g/3½ oz arrowroot

See **easy blending method** on page 9

Easy Blending Method

Weigh the ingredients.
Step 1

Place them into a large plastic bag and shake well. **Step 2 and 3**

Place a large sieve in another bag. **Step 4**

Shake the bag from side to side to sift the flour, press out any lumps. **Step 5**

The flour is now ready for use. Store in paper or cotton bags. Do not store in airtight containers. **Step 6**

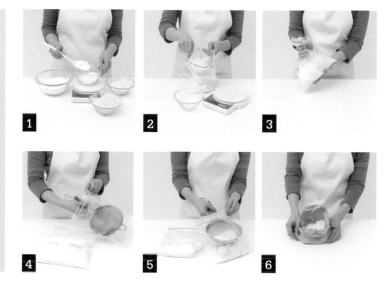

Sauce Blocks

I created these blocks years ago for my cookery classes to simplify sauce making. They have proved invaluable as a replacement for milk in producing a basic, dairy-free sauce that has many uses. This sauce can be used as a base for your own preservative-free baby food, to prevent quiche curdling in a hot oven, or to make a creamy dairy-free soup. Once you have tried them you will never be without them in your freezer.

200g/7 oz dairy-free margarine
  or 1 cup olive oil
200g/7 oz flour blend of choice (page 7)

1 Melt the margarine or heat oil in a saucepan over a low heat. Using a wooden spoon, stir in the flour.

2 Continue stirring and cook for about 3 minutes until the mixture slides in the saucepan.

3 Pour the mixture into a 12-cube icecube tray, then freeze until required.

Breakfast

We take for granted that breakfasts and brunches give us a great start to the day, especially if you do not have a problem with wheat based foods. But spare a thought for those who suffer a wheat or gluten allergy. This chapter has been written to give all of us a great start to the day, by providing alternatives to store bought breads and breakfast foods.

Amaranth Porridge

½ teaspoon salt
1 cup amaranth breakfast cereal
½ cup milk

1 Place 1½ cups of cold water and salt in a saucepan and bring to a boil. While stirring the water add the amaranth cereal in a steady stream.
2 Cook for about 2 minutes, add the milk, stir and cook until smooth.
3 Serve hot with stewed prunes and orange peel.

Amaranth cereal is made from the flowerets of a broad-leafed plant from South America. A centuries-old herb used by Aztecs and American Indians, it is higher in protein than wheat, corn or soya beans. According to the statistics on the packaging it is high in dietary fiber, as well as vitamins, calcium and many minerals. Apart from this it actually tastes good, with a mild nutty flavor so it is an ideal cereal for children, as well as adults.

Serves 1 • Preparation 5 minutes • Cooking 6 minutes

Polenta Porridge

½ cup fine polenta
½ cup milk
salt to taste

1 Place 1 cup of boiling water in a saucepan on high heat and boil rapidly.
   While briskly stirring the water with a wooden spoon, pour the polenta
   into the saucepan in a fine steady stream.
2 Continue stirring until it is thick and cooked, about 2 minutes. Stir in the
   milk and season with salt if desired. Season with salt as desired.

Serves 1 • Preparation 5 minutes • Cooking 8 minutes

Currant and Custard Rolls

1 batch of basic bun dough (page 64)
½ cup currants

Custard
2 tablespoons margarine
2 tablespoons Lola's superfine flour (page 7)
1 egg yolk
½ cup sugar
½ teaspoon vanilla extract
3 tablespoons almond meal

Glaze
1 teaspoon gelatin
2 tablespoons sugar

1 To make the custard, melt the margarine in a small saucepan and add the flour. Cook for 1 minute stirring with a wooden spoon. Add ½ cup of boiling water and cook until the custard is thick. Add the egg yolk, sugar, vanilla and almond meal, and stir well. It should be thick enough to hold its shape, if not add a little more almond meal.

2 Preheat the oven to 360°F/180°C. Oil a sheet of plastic wrap about 12 x 9 in/30 x 22cm. Cover a baking sheet with parchment paper. Press the dough out on the plastic wrap. Spread with the custard filling, and sprinkle with currants.

3 Roll the dough up lengthwise using the plastic wrap to help. Using an oiled knife, cut the rolls in thick slices and place on the prepared tray. Leave the rolls to rise for 20 minutes. Bake for 15 minutes.

4 To make the glaze, boil ingredients together with 2 tablespoon of water. Remove buns from oven and brush with glaze while still hot.

Serves 2–4 • Preparation 35 minutes • Cooking 20 minutes

Oven Baked Doughnuts

⅓ cup rice milk
2 teaspoons gelatin or agar powder
¼ teaspoon salt
1 teaspoon sugar
1 tablespoon dried yeast
3 egg whites
2 teaspoons vanilla extract
150g/5 oz powdered sugar
130g/4½ oz superfine flour (page 7)
60g/2 oz margarine, melted

1 Preheat the oven to 320°F/160°C. Grease a non-stick doughnut tray with margarine. Place the milk in a bowl, add the gelatin or agar, salt and sugar, then heat in a microwave for about 30 seconds until clear.
2 Stir in the dried yeast, then set aside to rise for a few minutes while you whisk the eggs, vanilla and powdered sugar to a stiff meringue.
3 Add the yeast mixture to the meringue. Using a wire whisk, blend in the flour and melted margarine.
4 Spoon into the greased doughnut cups. Let stand for 15 minutes, then bake for 12 minutes. Finish with cinnamon or powdered sugar as desired.

These doughnuts freeze well.

Serves 2–4 • Preparation 25 minutes • Cooking 12 minutes

Bacon and Egg Waffles

1 cup milk
160g/5½ oz superfine flour (page 7)
1 teaspoon gluten-free baking powder
¼ cup olive oil
¼ cup parsley, chopped
salt and freshly ground black pepper
2 slices bacon or ham, finely chopped
2 eggs

1 Brush the waffle iron with oil and heat to manufacturer's instructions. Place the milk into a bowl and sift in the flour and baking powder.

2 Mix with a whisk to ensure a smooth batter. Add the oil, parsley, salt and pepper. Add the bacon or ham to the batter.

3 Beat the eggs until light and fluffy and stir into the mixture. The batter should be very thin so that it will quickly and easily cover the waffle iron.

4 Pour mix into waffle iron and cook according to the manufacturer's instructions. Repeat until mix is all used, stirring prior to each pour to maintain consistency. These waffles freeze well wrapped in foil.

You will need an electric waffle iron to cook the waffles.

Serves 2 • Preparation 7 minutes • Cooking 5 minutes

Breakfast Bars

1 cup rolled rice flakes
1 tablespoon psyllium
½ cup dried apricots, chopped
1 tablespoon gluten-free baking powder
160g/5½ oz superfine flour (page 7)
1 cup puffed amaranth cereal
½ cup shredded coconut
½ cup cashew nuts, chopped
60g/2 oz ground sunflower kernels
1 cup golden raisins
2 tablespoons honey
125g/4 oz brown sugar
¼ cup olive oil
1 egg, beaten

1 Preheat the oven to 320°F/160°C. Line a 7 x 10 x 1 in/18 x 26 x 3cm deep baking pan with parchment paper. Place the rice flakes, psyllium, apricots and 2 cups of water in a covered microwave-safe dish and cook for 3 minutes in the microwave oven.

2 Add remaining ingredients to the cooked rice flake and apricot mixture. Stir well to combine ingredients and press into the pan and bake for 20 minutes.

3 Remove from oven, cut into bars, separate and place on a baking sheet. Return to oven and cook for an additional 20 minutes, let cool on the tray, then wrap and refrigerate until required.

This nutritious slice is perfect for a quick breakfast with a cup of coffee. It keeps well in the refrigerator for up to two weeks – a great stand by.

Serves 2 • Preparation 20 minutes • Cooking 45 minutes

Date and Ginger Granola Bars

½ cup whole grain rolled rice flakes
pinch salt
2 tablespoons rice or maple syrup
1 tablespoon sugar-free apricot jam
1 teaspoon almond extract
1 cup dates, chopped
120g/4 oz shredded coconut
60g/2 oz crystalized ginger, chopped
60g/2 oz ground almonds
2 tablespoons rice flour
1 tablespoon psyllium

1 Line a loaf pan with parchment paper. Place the rice flakes, salt and 200mL/7 oz of cold water into a deep microwave-safe dish. Cover and microwave on high for 3 minutes, then let stand for 3 minutes.

2 Add the rice flake mixture to other ingredients, mix well and press into the prepared pan. Bake for 20 minutes.

3 Remove from the oven and cut the mixture into four bars. Place the cut bars back into the oven on a baking sheet and bake for an additional 20 minutes, turning once. Let cool before wrapping.

These granola bars are great for breakfast on the go, or as a snack anytime. They will keep for at least two weeks in the refrigerator.

Makes 4 bars • Preparation 10 minutes • Cooking 50 minutes

French Toast

1 egg
¼ cup milk
2 slices bread

Savory Toast
salt and freshly ground black pepper

Sweet Toast
1 tablespoon sugar
1 teaspoon vanilla extract
½ teaspoon ground cinnamon

1 Whisk together the egg and milk. For savory toast, add salt and pepper to the mixture and whisk well. For sweet toast, add sugar, vanilla extract and cinnamon to the mixture and whisk well.
2 Melt a pat of butter in a frying pan. Dip the bread slices in the egg mixture, covering both sides. Place in the heated pan and cook for a few minutes, both sides over medium heat.
3 Serve with maple syrup or fruit.

Serves 1 • Preparation 7 minutes • Cooking 6 minutes

Potato Pancakes

1 egg
1 potato, unpeeled and coarsely grated
2 tablespoons superfine flour (page 7)
salt and freshly ground black pepper

1 Lightly whisk the egg and add to the grated potato. Fold in the flour, salt and
   pepper. Heat a small amount of oil in a shallow pan. Fry over a medium heat until
   golden, turning once. Sprinkle with kosher salt.

These crispy cakes are great with chopped bacon, ham, or green onion.

Serves 1 • Preparation 5 minutes • Cooking 5 minutes

Dairy-Free Pancakes

2 eggs
¼ cup lemonade or soda water
2 teaspoons vanilla extract
2 tablespoons olive oil
100g/3½ oz superfine flour (page 7)
2 tablespoons sugar
2 teaspoons gluten-free baking powder
½ cup extra oil to grease ring molds

1 Grease a flat pan or skillet with a little olive oil. Separate the eggs, put the two yolks in a medium-sized mixing bowl and retain the whites to beat separately.

2 Add the lemonade, vanilla extract and oil to the egg yolks. Combine the flour, sugar and baking powder and whisk in the liquids using a wire whisk. Set aside.

3 Whisk the two egg whites with a rotary or electric beater until stiff. Stir the stiffened egg into the pancake batter and whisk well. Pour into a pitcher for easier handling while cooking.

4 Place some oil in a small pie tin to oil the ring molds. Heat the pan on medium heat. Pour about half a cupful of batter into ring molds in the greased pan. Let cook until the batter is set. Turn once to cook other side.

5 Serve warm with honey or syrup. These hotcakes freeze well in a plastic container or wrapped in foil.

Free of corn, wheat, soy, gluten and dairy, I use ring molds to regulate the size of the pancakes as they are made from a thin batter. If you don't have ring molds use a small omelette pan.

Serves 1 • Preparation 10 minutes • Cooking 7 minutes

Crêpes

1 egg
1 cup milk
100g/3½ oz Lola's all-purpose flour (page 7)
1 tablespoon olive oil
juice of ½ lemon

1 Beat the egg and half the milk together. Add the sifted flour and the oil and beat until a smooth batter forms. Thin with the remainder of the milk. Let stand for a few minutes and adjust the consistency to a thin batter with additional water if required. Finally, add the lemon juice. Let stand while you prepare the crêpe pan.

2 Melt 1 teaspoon of butter in a non-stick pan. Wipe out with paper towel and grease again with a small amount of butter. Adjust the heat under the pan to a low temperature. This important step will ensure even cooking of the crêpes with any pan, even one with a non-stick surface.

3 Pour a very thin layer of batter into the pan and then tilt the pan quickly to give a good coverage. By the time the pan is covered the crêpe should be set, if not the batter is too thick. To correct, add a little more water.

4 With a spatula, carefully ease the crêpe from the edge of the pan and flip it over to cook the other side for a few seconds.

As each crêpe is cooked, slide it onto a plate or piece of foil and cover with a cloth to prevent drying.

Makes 1½ cups pancake mix • Preparation 10 minutes • Cooking 10 minutes

Fluffy Pancakes

2 eggs
2 tablespoons olive oil
1 teaspoon vanilla extract
¼ cup lemonade or warm water
100g/3½ oz Lola's all-purpose flour (page 7)
2 level teaspoons gluten-free baking powder
1 tablespoon psyllium
2 tablespoons milk powder

1 Separate the eggs, place the yolks in a large bowl and whites in a small bowl to be beaten later. Add the olive oil, vanilla extract and lemonade or water to the yolks and whisk lightly. Whisk the dry ingredients into the liquid mixture. Beat the egg whites until firm and whisk into the batter. Let rest as you prepare the pan.

2 Melt 1 teaspoon of butter in a small pan. Wipe out with paper towel and grease again with a small amount of butter. Adjust the heat under the pan to a low temperature. This important step will ensure even cooking of the cakes with any pan, even one with a non-stick surface.

3 Regulate the heat to low under the prepared pan. Place a small amount of batter into the pan using a ladle or a small pitcher to pour the batter. If the mixture is too thick to pour, add a little more warm water. Cook the cake until it starts to bubble and looks firm on top. Turn with a spatula and cook for just a few seconds on the other side. Remove from the pan and keep covered with foil or a cloth until ready for use.

Even non-stick pans need to be seasoned to cook pancakes made with gluten-free flour. An electric frypan needs only a light oiling as the heat is regulated.

Serves 2 • Preparation 12 minutes • Cooking 8 minutes

Buckwheat Pancakes

2 tablespoons egg substitute
2 teaspoons agar powder
2 tablespoons olive oil
90g/3 oz Lola's all-purpose flour (page 7)
2 tablespoons buckwheat flour
2 teaspoons gluten-free baking powder
2 tablespoons rice milk

1 Beat the egg substitute, agar and ⅓ cup warm water with an electric beater until frothy then continue beating until thick and creamy. Using a wire whisk, fold in the oil, flours and baking powder. Add the rice milk and whisk well until the mixture is a smooth batter. It should be thin enough to pour and cover the bottom of the pan – if not add a little more warm water.

2 Grease a flat pan or skillet and place it on a medium heat. Pour in enough mixture to thinly coat the bottom of the pan. Lift the pan and tilt to help spread the mixture evenly over the pan base.

3 Cook until the top is firm. Turn with a spatula and cook the other side. Cover with a cloth or place in a plastic bag to prevent drying. The pancakes will freeze well wrapped in foil. Thaw before reheating to serve.

Serves 2 • Preparation 8 minutes • Cooking 8 minutes

Crumpets

1 teaspoon sugar
1 teaspoon salt
1 tablespoon dried yeast
1 tablespoon psyllium
1 tablespoon olive oil
250g/8 oz Lola's bread and pastry flour (page 7)
3 teaspoons gluten-free baking powder

1　Place 1 cup of warm water, sugar and salt in a bowl and stir in the yeast. Let stand for about 5 minutes or until bubbles appear and the mixture is frothy. In another bowl, add the psyllium to ¼ cup cold water and let stand until it becomes a jelly. Pour a few tablespoons of oil onto a plate and grease ring molds.

2　Combine the yeast and psyllium mixtures and add the olive oil and flour. Finally, add the baking powder and beat well with an electric mixer to distribute the yeast – if the mixture is too thick to pour, add a little more warm water.

3　Heat a large skillet or griddle on medium heat, add a little oil and place greased ring molds into the pan. Pour enough batter into the ring mold to fill it halfway. Cook until the crumpet starts to bubble and set. Using tongs, carefully remove the ring and continue to cook on low heat until set. Turn and cook until lightly browned (You can also cover with a lid to cook without having to turn). Repeat with remaining batter.

4　Serve toasted with butter or honey. Crumpets will keep for a week in the refrigerator.

Serves 2 • Preparation 15 minutes • Cooking 15 minutes

Veggie Frittata

3 or 4 large mushrooms
1 russet or Idaho potato, unpeeled and sliced
½ cup peas, chopped peppers

Basic Sauce
2 sauce blocks (page 9)
salt and freshly ground black pepper
3 beaten eggs or substitute

1 Preheat broiler. To make the basic sauce, place 1 cup of boiling water in the saucepan, add the sauce blocks and let stand until soft. Return to the heat and whisk until it thickens. Season with salt and pepper. Remove from the heat and add the beaten eggs or substitute. Set aside.

2 In a large skillet, on medium heat, melt a tablespoon of dairy-free margarine. Cook potatoes until browned and tender. Remove to a plate. Saute mushrooms and peppers (if using).

3 Add potatoes to pan and spread vegetables in an even layer. Pour the reserved sauce over the vegetables, and cook on low heat for about 5–10 minutes until set. Broil for 1–2 minutes to set the mixture. Serve immediately.

Frittatas are a great way to use leftover meat and vegetables. Get creative with spinach, onions, and fresh herbs.

Serves 2 • Preparation 8 minutes • Cooking 15 minutes

Muffins and Quick Breads

Many enterprising home bakers have started businesses baking gluten free biscuits, cakes etc, which is great news if you know where they are located. In addition some home based companies are now producing ready-to-bake bread, muffins and biscuit mixes. However, with this book you will able to make your own with the best of them!

Bush Damper

1 tablespoon psyllium
1 egg
2 teaspoons milk or water for egg wash
200g/7 oz superfine flour (page 7)
2 tablespoons milk powder
1 tablespoon gluten-free baking powder
1 teaspoon salt

1 Preheat oven to 430°F/220°C. Grease a baking sheet or line with parchment paper. Place ¼ cup of cold water in a small bowl and sprinkle the psyllium on top. Whisk lightly and leave to gel for about 3 minutes.

2 To make the egg wash without using an additional egg – lightly whisk the egg in a small mixing bowl. Tip the egg into a large mixing bowl to use in the damper mixture, then add 2 teaspoons of milk or water to the small bowl. Wash around the bowl with the pastry brush and you have egg wash to glaze the damper.

3 To the egg add ¼ cup of warm water and psyllium mix. Place the flour, milk powder, baking powder and salt in a plastic bag and shake well. Add three quarters of the flour mixture to the egg mixture and fold with a table knife to combine into a soft dough. Do not mix more than necessary.

4 Place the remaining flour mixture on a board in a well shape. Tip the soft dough into the well. Knead very quickly a few times to combine all the ingredients. Shape into a damper and mark sections with a knife. Place on the baking sheet and glaze with the egg wash. Cook on a high shelf in the oven for about 15 minutes. Remove from the oven and cool on a wire rack covered with a damp kitchen towel.

Serves 2 • Preparation 25 minutes • Cooking 15 minutes

Pumpkin Scones

1 tablespoon psyllium
1 egg
1 tablespoon milk for egg wash
½ cup olive oil
1 tablespoon honey
60g/2 oz cooked mashed pumpkin
300g/10½ oz Lola's all-purpose flour (page 7)
2 tablespoons milk powder
1 teaspoon nutmeg
2 tablespoons gluten-free baking powder
1 teaspoon salt

1 Preheat the oven to 440°F/220°C. Grease a baking sheet or line with parchment paper. Add the psyllium to ¼ cup cold water and let stand to form a jelly.

2 To make egg wash without using an additional egg, lightly whisk the egg in a small mixing bowl, then tip the egg into a large mixing bowl to use in the scone mixture. Add 1 teaspoon milk to the small bowl, mix to combine with the egg residue with the pastry brush and you have egg wash to glaze the scones.

3 Add the oil and honey to the mashed pumpkin and stir in the psyllium jelly, egg and 2 tablespoons hot water. Place the flour, milk powder, nutmeg, baking powder and salt into the mixture and fold with a table knife to combine to a soft dough. Do not mix more than necessary.

4 Place a little extra flour on a piece of plastic wrap, tip the soft scone dough on to it, cover with wrap and knead gently. Uncover. Lightly oil your fingers and press into a thick slab, and cut into six thick scones. Place on the baking sheet and brush with egg wash. Bake on the highest oven rack for 15–20 minutes. Remove from oven and wrap in a damp kitchen towel to cool.

Serves 2 • Preparation 25 minutes • Cooking 20 minutes

Scones

1 tablespoon psyllium
1 egg
2 tablespoons butter
250g/8 oz Lola's bread and pastry flour (page 7)
1 tablespoon gluten-free baking powder
100g/3½ oz arrowroot
2 teaspoons gelatin
2 tablespoons pure icing sugar

1 Preheat the oven to 400°F/200°C. Grease a baking sheet or line with parchment paper. Add the psyllium ¼ cup of cold water and let stand to form a jelly.

2 To make an eggwash without using an additional egg, lightly whisk the egg in a small mixing bowl, then tip the egg into the psyllium mixture. Add 2 teaspoons of water to the mixing bowl, mix to combine.

3 Lightly whisk the egg and psyllium mixture, then add ½ cup warm water and butter. Continue mixing, then add the remaining dry ingredients. Combine well with a knife and if still too sticky turn out onto a floured cutting board to knead in a little extra flour, or fine rice flour.

4 Cut out using an oiled cutter and place on the prepared tray, glaze with egg wash and bake for 10–15 minutes. Wrap in a kitchen towel to cool.

Serves 2 • Preparation 20 minutes • Cooking 15 minutes

Mixed Berry Muffins

3 tablespoons sugar
1 tablespoon psyllium
1 tablespoon gelatin
1 tablespoon dried yeast
2 egg whites
1 teaspoon salt
½ teaspoon citric acid
250g/8 oz superfine flour (page 7)
2 tablespoons olive oil
1 cup mixed berries

1 Grease a muffin tin or line the pan with cupcake liners. Place 1 cup of cold water into a large glass bowl or microwave dish. Add the sugar, psyllium and gelatin. Let stand for 1 minute to soften.

2 Heat the gelatin mixture in the microwave for 50 seconds. Add the yeast and let stand for 10 minutes. Whisk the egg whites, salt and citric acid in a separate bowl with an electric mixer until stiff. Fold the dry ingredients into the wet mixture.

3 Beat in the oil and whisked eggs for 1 minute with electric mixer. Cover and let stand again for 10 minutes.

4 Preheat the oven to 360°F/180°C. Spoon a tablespoon of the mixture into each cup, sprinkle with half the fruit, add more batter, then sprinkle with remaining fruit, top with mixture and leave until puffy – about 15 minutes. Place in the center of the oven and bake for 20 minutes. Remove from the oven and wrap in a clean kitchen towel to cool, remove muffins from the pans, then place in a plastic bag until ready to serve.

Makes 8 • Preparation 35 minutes • Cooking 22 minutes

Banana Blueberry Muffins

200mL/7 oz milk
1 teaspoon salt
1 tablespoon gelatin
100g/3½ oz sugar
1 tablespoon dried yeast
2 eggs
1 ripe banana
2 tablespoons rice syrup or honey
2 tablespoons olive oil
160g/6 oz superfine flour (page 7)
1 tablespoon psyllium
1 cup fresh blueberries

1 Grease a 12-cup muffin tin or line the pan with cupcake liners. Place milk in a large microwave-proof mixing bowl. Add salt, gelatin and 1 tablespoon of the sugar. Let stand for a few minutes, and then heat in microwave for 1 minute on high.

2 Stir the yeast into the warm milk mixture and let stand for 20 minutes. Lightly beat the eggs. In a small bowl, mash the banana and add the rice syrup, olive oil and eggs. Blend this mixture until smooth.

3 Combine the two wet mixes in the large bowl and add the flour, psyllium, and remaining sugar. Mix well, cover the bowl and let rise for 20 minutes.

4 Preheat the oven to 360°F/180°C. Fold in the blueberries and spoon the mixture into the muffin tins. Let rise for another 20 minutes before baking. Bake muffins for 30 minutes. Remove from oven and wrap in a clean kitchen towel to cool.

Makes 12 • Preparation 1 hour 15 minutes • Cooking 30 minutes

Banana Muffins

1 tablespoon egg substitute
2 teaspoons gelatin or agar powder
1 very ripe banana
2 tablespoons olive oil
100g/3½ oz sugar
150g/5 oz flour blend of choice (page 7)
2 teaspoons vanilla extract
2 teaspoons gluten-free baking powder
1 teaspoon baking soda

1 Preheat the oven to 360°F/180°C. Line a muffin tin with cupcake liners. Place ⅓ cup warm water in a bowl with the egg substitute and gelatin or agar. Let stand while you mash the banana and oil together.

2 Beat the egg substitute mixture until thick. Gradually add the sugar and continue beating until the consistency of a thick meringue.

3 Fold in the banana and oil and then the flour, vanilla, baking powder and baking soda, using a wire whisk to produce a cupcake mixture that will hold its shape.

4 Fill each liner with batter, about three-quarters full. Bake for 15 minutes.

Serves 2–4 • Preparation 15 minutes • Cooking 15 minutes

High-Fiber Carrot Cake

200g/7 oz Lola's all-purpose flour (page 7)
2 teaspoons gluten-free baking powder
1 tablespoons gelatin
1 tablespoon psyllium
2 teaspoons pumpkin pie spice
60g/2 oz shredded coconut
125g/4 oz finely grated carrot
125g/4 oz golden raisins
170g/6 oz brown sugar
½ cup olive oil
2 teaspoons vanilla extract
3 eggs

Lemon Frosting
250g/8 oz sifted powdered sugar
1 tablespoon butter
1 tablespoon lemon juice

1 Preheat the oven to 360°F/180°C. Grease a 10 x 7 x 2 in/26 x 18 x 5cm loaf pan and line the bottom with parchment paper. Lightly whisk the eggs.

2 Combine the flour, baking powder, gelatin, psyllium, spices, coconut, carrot and golden raisins. Place the brown sugar, oil and vanilla in a large saucepan and warm slightly. Remove from the heat and add all the other ingredients, alternating the dry ingredients with the eggs. Combine well and spoon into the loaf pan.

3 Bake the center of the oven for 25 minutes. Let cool in the pan.

4 To make the lemon frosting, whisk ingredients together well and use to top the cooled cake.

Serves 2–4 • Preparation 20 minutes • Cooking 25 minutes

Pumpkin Pan Bread

1 teaspoon sugar
2 teaspoons gelatin
1 teaspoon salt
2 teaspoons dried yeast
2 tablespoons warm mashed pumpkin
200g/7 oz flour blend of choice (page 7)
2 tablespoons olive oil

1 Place ½ cup warm water in a medium mixing bowl and add the sugar, gelatin, salt and yeast. Stir in the mashed pumpkin and let rise for 10 minutes.

2 Add three-quarters of the flour to the yeast and mix well. Place the remaining flour on a board and tip the dough onto it. Knead lightly until all the flour is absorbed. Oil the bowl the bread was mixed in with 1 tablespoon of olive oil.

3 Place the dough back in the bowl and roll it around in the oil to cover the surface. Cover with a cloth and let rest for 20 minutes.

4 Remove dough from the bowl and on a chopping board, form a flat circle of dough to fit the base of your frying pan. If too sticky, use a little fine rice flour and knead into the dough.

5 Oil the pan with the remaining olive oil. Heat your pan to a medium heat and lift the dough and tip it into the pan. Adjust the size if necessary by pressing out a little more with your fingers.

6 Cut the dough into quarters with a knife. Cook the bread for 3 minutes over medium heat before turning with a spatula. Reduce pan heat to low and continue to cook for an additional 10 minutes until the bread sounds hollow when tapped.

Serves 2 • Preparation 30 minutes • Cooking 15 minutes

Orange Poppyseed Cake

3 eggs
150g/5 oz sugar
150g/5 oz Lola's all-purpose flour (page 7)
90g/3 oz ground almonds
zest of 2 oranges
2 tablespoons psyllium
1 tablespoon gelatin
2 tablespoons poppy seeds
2 teaspoons gluten-free baking powder
150g/5 oz butter
½ cup orange juice

Orange Icing
2 cups powdered sugar
juice of 1 orange
2 tablespoons butter or margarine

1 Preheat the oven to 360°F/180°C. Generously grease a 12 in/30cm loaf pan with margarine. Place all the ingredients into a mixing bowl in their listed order and mix well with an electric mixer for about 1 minute and scrape into the prepared pan.

2 Bake on the middle rack of the oven, until just firm to the touch, about 35 minutes. Remove from the oven and drizzle the warm cake with orange juice while it's still in the pan. Wait a few minutes before removing from the pan.

3 Cream butter, powdered sugar and orange juice together until smooth. Spread on the cooled cake. Cake will keep for several days in an air-tight container.

Serves 2–4 • Preparation 15 minutes • Cooking 35 minutes

Apple Spice Bread

1 teaspoon salt
3 tablespoons sugar
1 tablespoon gelatin
60g/2 oz mashed potatoes
1 tablespoon dry yeast
200g/7 oz Lola's bread and pastry flour (page 7)
75g/2½ oz arrowroot
1 tablespoon ground ginger
1 tablespoon pumpkin pie spice
1 teaspoon cinnamon
2 eggs
1 chopped apple
150g/5 oz golden raisins

1 Grease a loaf or bundt pan with some dairy-free margarine. Place 200mL/7 oz cold water into a glass bowl. Add the salt, sugar and gelatin; let stand for 1 minute to soften. Heat the gelatin mixture in the microwave for 30 seconds or until gelatin dissolves.
2 Whisk the mashed potatoes into the warm gelatin mixture. Stir in the yeast and let stand for 3 minutes. Combine the flour, arrowroot and spices. Tip the dry ingredients into the wet mixture and beat in the whisked eggs. Beat the mixture for 1 minute with the electric mixer.
3 Preheat oven to 360°F/180°C. Pour a quarter of the mixture into the bread pan and spread over the base. Sprinkle a quarter of the apple and raisins over the mixture and top with more batter. Cover the remaining fruit with more dough mixture. Let stand for 15 minutes. Place in the center of the oven and bake for 35 minutes. Remove from the oven and wrap in a kitchen towel and leave to cool.

Serves 2–4 • Preparation 40 minutes • Cooking 35 minutes

Breads and Rolls

Remember when making bread, that homemade bread is not meant to keep fresh more than one day. The ingredients added to commercial breads to extend shelf-life have chemicals and additional gluten, these are ingredients we want to avoid. You will find that once organized, you will enjoy the challenge of producing fresh, chemical-free foods.

Cornish Splits

1 teaspoon psyllium
1 teaspoon salt
1 tablespoon dried yeast
1 egg
450g/16 oz superfine flour (page 7)
30g/1 oz powdered sugar, sifted
2 tablespoons powdered milk
1 tablespoon margarine, melted

1 Preheat the oven to 400°F/200°C. Line a baking sheet with parchment paper. Place ½ cup of warm water in a large mixing bowl and whisk in the psyllium, salt and yeast. Set aside to rise for 10 minutes while you prepare the other ingredients. In a small bowl whisk the egg. Weigh the flour and set aside 150g/5 oz of it for rolling the splits.

2 Combine the larger portion of flour with the icing sugar and powdered milk. Add the beaten egg and melted margarine to the yeast mixture. Set the bowl aside to make egg wash by adding a teaspoon of milk and combining with egg residue.

3 Using a knife to avoid over-mixing add the flour mixture to the liquids and blend using a cutting action for about 1 minute until the flour is incorporated. Cover the bowl and let rest for 15 minutes.

4 Add half the remaining flour to the risen dough and work in with the knife. Place the remainder of the flour on a pastry board and tip the dough on it. Lightly knead to incorporate the flour, adding a little more flour if necessary. Press the dough out in a thick slab with your fingers and cut with a small cutter.

5 Place the splits next to each other on the baking sheet, so sides touch when the bake. Brush the tops with egg wash and let rise for 40 minutes. Bake for 15 minutes until golden.

Traditionally from Cornwall, England, these slightly sweet white rolls are served warm with tea, spread with butter, strawberry jam and clotted cream.

Serves 2 • Preparation 1 hour 10 minutes • Cooking 15 minutes

Panettone

1 tablespoon dried yeast
100g/3½ oz sugar
200g/7 oz superfine flour (page 7)
2 eggs, separated
½ teaspoon salt
60g/2 oz softened butter
2 teaspoons vanilla extract
125g/4 oz golden raisins
60g/2 oz candied citrus fruit or citron

1 Grease a deep 8-inch round cake pan or can with margarine. Dissolve yeast in ½ cup of warm water with 1 tablespoon of the sugar and half the flour. Mix well, cover and allow to rise until puffy – about 20 minutes.

2 Beat egg whites, salt and remaining sugar until stiff and add to the dough, alternating with remainder of the flour.

3 Add egg yolks and softened butter then beat with electric mixer for 2 minutes. Cover and let mixture rise again until doubled, about 20 minutes. Punch down and add the vanilla.

4 Preheat the oven to 320°F/160°C. Pour a little mixture into pan, add golden raisins and citron then more mixture, continuing this method until all the fruit and mixture is used. Allow mixture to stand for about 30 minutes or until the pan is three-parts full. Cook for 40 minutes on the lowest backing rack.

Cooked in a traditional tall can, this Italian yeast cake is served with coffee at breakfast throughout the year and is a popular gift at Christmas. It also works beautifully in large cans for individual loaves.

Serves 2–4 • Preparation 1 hour 15 minutes • Cooking 40 minutes

Potato Bread

1 tablespoon gelatin
60g/2 oz soft mashed potato
60g/2 oz arrowroot
¼ cup olive oil
1 teaspoon sugar
1 teaspoon salt
1 tablespoon dried yeast
200g/7 oz Lola's bread and pastry flour (page 7)
1 tablespoon baby rice cereal or extra arrowroot
1 egg
2 teaspoons sesame seeds

1 Preheat the oven to 400°F/200°C. Place the gelatin into 200mL/7 oz of cold water and let stand to soften. Select a 9 x 3 x 3 in/23 x 8 x 7cm loaf pan to cook the loaf. Bread cooks best in tin, not aluminium.

2 When the gelatin has softened, heat the mixture over low heat until clear. Tip the hot gelatin mixture into the mashed potato and arrowroot and mix well. Add the olive oil, sugar and salt to this mixture and while it is still warm add the yeast.

3 Sift in the flour, baby rice cereal and the beaten egg. Beat the mixture with a rotary beater or whisk. The mixture should be a thick batter – add more warm water if too stiff. Pour the batter into the prepared pan and let it stand for about 15 minutes until bubbles are rising to the surface. Sprinkle with sesame seeds and place in the center of the oven.

4 Cook for about 40 minutes or until the loaf sounds hollow when tapped.

This mixture is meant to be a quick, easy bread for eating the same day as baked as. If you wish to keep it longer or freeze it, beat it again after the initial 15 minute rise and let it rise again, then beat and leave for another 20 minutes before baking.

Serves 2–4 • Preparation 30 minutes • Cooking 45 minutes

Mini White Loaves

1 tablespoon dried yeast
1 tablespoon sugar
1 tablespoon gelatin
1 teaspoon salt
1 tablespoon psyllium
½ teaspoon citric acid
300g/10½ oz superfine flour (page 7)
2 egg whites

1 Grease a 7 x 4 x 3 in/18 x 11 x 10cm loaf pan with margarine and line with parchment paper. Place ½ cup of hot water and ½ cup of cold, into a medium-sized glass or plastic bowl. Add the yeast, sugar, gelatin, salt and psyllium. Lightly whisk to mix ingredients. Cover the bowl and leave to rise for 15 minutes.

2 Add the flour, citric acid and egg whites to the yeast mixture and mix for 2 minutes, using an electric beater. Cover the bowl with a large plastic bag and let rise for 20 minutes. Beat the mixture for 1 minute and scrape into the prepared loaf pan.

3 Preheat oven to 440°F/220°C. Cover the pan with the plastic bag and let rise for 25 minutes or less until the mixture is 1 in/25mm from the top of the tin.

4 Bake on the lowest baking rack for 40 minutes. Remove from oven and wrap in a clean kitchen towel. Do not cut until cool.

There is no oil in this loaf so it doesn't freeze for long.

Serves 2 • Preparation 50 minutes • Cooking 40 minutes

Sunflower Bread

2 tablespoons gelatin
2 teaspoons sugar
2 teaspoons salt
450g/16 oz superfine flour (page 7)
60g/2 oz brown rice flour
2 tablespoons dried yeast
3 egg whites
60g/2 oz sunflower meal
¼ cup olive oil

1 Grease a heavy 11 x 5 x 4 in/28 x 12 x 10cm loaf pan with margarine and line with parchment paper. Place 2 cups of cold water into large mixing bowl, add the gelatin, sugar and salt and stand for 2 minutes to soften the gelatin.

2 Heat the gelatin mixture for approximately 1 minute until clear. Add the flour, rice flour and yeast to the warm liquid and beat with an electric mixer for about 1 minute.

3 Cover the bowl with a large plastic bag and let rise for 10 minutes. Whisk the egg whites in a separate bowl until stiff. Add the beaten egg whites, sunflower meal and oil to the bread mixture and beat for about 2 minutes.

4 Preheat the oven to 400°F/200°C. Pour the mixture into the prepared loaf pan and leave to rise for 20–25 minutes until about 1 in/25mm from the top of the pan. Bake on the lowest baking rack of the oven for 1 hour. Remove from oven and wrap in a clean kitchen towel. Do not cut until cold.

This loaf freezes well – it is better to slice it before freezing. An electric knife is very good for slicing gluten-free bread. The grainy texture is achieved by the addition of sunflower meal made by blending sunflower kernels for a few minutes.

Serves 2–4 • Preparation 35 minutes • Cooking 1 hour

Sourdough Bread

Starter for Sourdough
2 tablespoons dried yeast
180g/6½ oz superfine flour (page 7)
1 teaspoon sugar
1 teaspoon salt

Bread
125mL/4 oz sourdough starter (see above)
200g/7 oz superfine flour (page 7)
1 teaspoon salt
1 teaspoon sugar
1 teaspoon dried yeast
1 egg

1 To make the starter for the sourdough, place all starter ingredients, plus 1 cup of lukewarm water in a jar and leave for at least 48 hours. Stir twice daily. Use up to a third of mixture to make sourdough bread. Replace used starter with equal quantities of flour and water and do not use again for another 48 hours.

2 Preheat the oven to 360°F/180°C. To make the bread, select and grease a loaf pan. Place the starter in a medium-sized bowl add 125mL/4 oz warm water and all the other ingredients. Beat with an electric mixer for 2 minutes. Pour into the greased pan and allow to rise for 30 minutes. Place on the lowest baking rack in the oven and bake for 40 minutes. Cool and refrigerate before slicing.

It's best to use a deep loaf pan for this recipe because it only rises once, creating a coarse texture. For a more refined texture, punch down the dough after it has risen 15 minutes, then let rise another 30 minutes.

Serves 2–4 • Preparation 40 minutes • Cooking 40 minutes

Sandwich Bread

2 tablespoons gelatin
3 egg whites
1 teaspoon sugar
2 tablespoons dried yeast
1 teaspoon salt
450g/16 oz Lola's bread and pastry flour (page 7)
60g/2 oz arrowroot
½ cup olive oil

1 Grease a deep loaf pan 11 x 5 x 4 in/28 x 12 x 10cm and line it with parchment paper. Place the gelatin into 1 cup of the cold water and let it soak until it sinks. Heat the gelatin mixture until it is clear. Set aside to cool. Place ½ cup of cold water and ½ cup boiling water in a small bowl and add the sugar and yeast. It will become frothy in a few minutes.

2 Whisk the egg whites with the salt until stiff. While beating the egg whites, add the gelatin mixture a spoonful at a time. Remove from the mixer, sift the flour and arrowroot into the egg mixture and fold in the frothy yeast, then the oil.

3 Whisk the mixture to ensure that the ingredients are blended. Cover the basin with plastic wrap and leave the bread mixture to stand in the basin for about 15 minutes until the mixture is puffy – the time is dependent on the quality of the yeast.

4 Preheat the oven to 400°F/200°C. Whisk the dough and repeat the process for a second rising. Whisk again and pour into the prepared loaf pan. Cover and let stand for 20–30 minutes to rise, until it is about an 1 in/2½cm from top of pan – it will continue to rise in the oven.

5 Place the bread on the lowest rack in your oven and after 10 minutes place a cookie sheet on top of the pan to give a square sandwich loaf that is easy to slice. Bake the bread for 1 hour. Remove from the oven and cool in the tin before slicing.

Serves 2–4 • Preparation 50 minutes • Cooking 1 hour 10 minutes

Amaranth Wraps

2 tablespoons egg substitute
1 teaspoon salt
150g/5 oz flour blend of choice (page 7)
1 teaspoon gluten-free baking powder
3 tablespoons olive oil
1 tablespoon amaranth cereal

1 Beat the egg substitute, salt (if using) and 1 cup warm water with an electric beater until frothy. Stir in the flour, baking powder and oil.
2 Whisk well until the mixture is a thin smooth batter, then stir in the amaranth cereal. Allow to stand while you prepare the pan. The mixture should be thin enough to pour – if too thick add a little more warm water.
3 Heat the pan to a medium heat and oil lightly. Pour about a cup of the mixture into the pan. Spread well to form a large circle and cook for a few minutes until set. Loosen with a spatula and turn to cook the other side – about 2 minutes. Allow to cool for a minute or two. Remove from pan and cover with foil or place in a plastic bag.
4 Store in the refrigerator and warm before filling to prevent crumbling.

These wraps are cooked in a frying pan, but you can cook them in the oven on a pizza tray or in smaller pans. The amount of mixture should be amended to suit the size of the pan.

Makes 3 wraps • Preparation 25 minutes • Cooking 20 minutes

Yeast-Free Saddle Loaf

1 teaspoon gelatin
2 tablespoons sesame seeds
1 tablespoon glycerine
250g/8 oz superfine flour (page 7)
3 teaspoons gluten-free baking powder
2 egg whites
½ teaspoon salt
1 tablespoon olive oil

1 Place ¼ cup of cold water in a small bowl and sprinkle the gelatin over it. Let stand until the gelatin sinks. Heat the mixture until the gelatin dissolves. Grease the loaf pan and line it with parchment paper or sprinkle with seeds. Place ½ cup of warm water into a small bowl with the glycerine. Place the flour and baking powder into a large bowl and mix well.

2 Beat the egg whites and salt until stiff. Spoon the warm gelatin mixture into the egg whites, a little at a time while beating. Pour the warm glycerine mixture into the beaten egg whites, add the dry ingredients and fold the mixture with a large wire whisk.

3 Preheat oven to 400°F/200°C. Whisk again and add the oil and an extra 2 tablespoons of warm water. Check the consistency – it should pour like custard, add more water if necessary. Pour into the prepared loaf pan and cover with plastic wrap. Let stand for 10 minutes. Cook loaf in the center of the oven for 40 minutes. Remove from the pan and wrap in a damp cloth until cold.

This dough can be pressed into a square baking dish for a foccacia loaf, or shaped into hamburger buns.

Serves 2–4 • Preparation 25 minutes • Cooking 45 minutes

Butternut Squash Bread

1 tablespoon gelatin
1 teaspoon sugar
1 teaspoon salt
pumpkin seeds
1 tablespoon dried yeast
250g/8 oz superfine flour (page 7)
2 egg yolks, or 1 egg, or egg substitute
½ cup olive oil
60g/2 oz butternut squash, grated

1 Preheat the oven to 400°F/200°C. Place the gelatin, sugar and salt into 200mL/7 oz
   of cold water and let stand for about 2 minutes to soften the gelatin. Grease a
   12 x 3 in/30 x 8cm loaf pan well with margarine and sprinkle with pumpkin seeds.

2 When the gelatin has softened heat the mixture for 1 minute and while it is
   still warm add the yeast. Let sit for 10 minutes. Sift in the flour and egg or egg-
   substitute mixture. Add the oil and beat the mixture with an electric beater for
   about 1 minute. The mixture should be a thick batter. Add a little more warm
   water if too stiff.

3 Pour a thin layer of the batter into the prepared tin and sprinkle about one third
   of the grated squash over it. Repeat the method until all the batter and squash
   is used. Let the mixture rise in the pan for 10–15 minutes, or until the mixture is
   ½ in/ 1¼cm form the top of the pan. It will continue to rise in the oven.

4 Cook for about 40 minutes or until the loaf sounds hollow when tapped.

Serves 2–4 • Preparation 40 minutes • Cooking 40 minutes

Herb and Onion Bread

1 tablespoon gelatin
1 teaspoon sugar
1 teaspoon salt
1 tablespoon sesame seeds
1 tablespoon dried yeast
250g/8 oz superfine flour (page 7)
1 egg
½ cup olive oil
1 tablespoon dried onion
1 teaspoon fresh or dried herbs

1 Preheat the oven to 400°F/200°C. Place the gelatin, sugar and salt into 200mL/7 oz of cold water and let stand for about 2 minutes to soften the gelatin. Grease a 12 x 3 in/30 x 8cm loaf pan well with margarine and sprinkle with sesame seeds. When the gelatin has softened heat the mixture for 30 seconds and add the yeast. Stand for 10 minutes to proof the yeast.

2 Sift in the flour. Add the egg and oil and beat the mixture with an electric mixer for about 1 minute. The mixture should be a thick batter. Add a little more warm water if too stiff. Fold in the dried onion and herbs and pour into the prepared tin.

3 Let the mixture rise in the pan for 10–15 minutes, or until mixture is ½ in/1¼cm form top of the pan. It will continue to rise in the oven.

4 Cook for about 40 minutes or until the loaf sounds hollow when tapped.

Serves 2 • Preparation 30 minutes • Cooking 40 minutes

Hamburger Buns

2 tablespoons gelatin
2 teaspoons sugar
2 teaspoons salt
500g/17½ oz superfine flour (page 7)
2 tablespoons dried yeast
3 egg whites
½ teaspoon citric acid
½ cup olive oil

1 Preheat the oven to 400°F/200°C. Grease three extra large muffin tin with margarine. Place 2 cups of cold water into a large mixing bowl and add the gelatin, sugar and salt. Stand for 2 minutes to soften the gelatin. Heat the gelatin mixture for approximately 1 minute until clear. Add the flour and yeast to the warm liquid and beat with an electric mixer for about 1 minute.

2 Cover the bowl with a large plastic bag. Let rise for 10 minutes. Whisk the egg whites and citric acid in a separate bowl until stiff. Add the beaten egg whites and oil to the bread mixture and beat for about 2 minutes.

3 Pour the mixture into the prepared pans and leave to rise for 10–15 minutes until they are puffy. Bake on the middle rack of the oven for 15 minutes. Remove from oven and wrap in a clean kitchen towel. Do not cut until cold.

Serves 2–4 • Preparation 40 minutes • Cooking 15 minutes

Poppy Seed Loaf

4 tablespoons poppy seeds
1 tablespoon gelatin
2 teaspoons salt
2 teaspoons sugar
125g/4 oz warm mashed potatoes
¼ cup olive oil
2 tablespoons dried yeast
500g/17½ oz superfine flour (page 7)
2 eggs

1 Preheat the oven to 400°F/200°C. Grease 4 mini loaf pans with margarine. Line the bottoms with 1 tablespoon of poppy seeds. Place the gelatin, salt and sugar in 2 cups of cold water and let stand for 2 minutes.

2 When the gelatin has softened heat the mixture until clear. Tip the hot gelatin mixture into the mashed potato and mix well. Add the olive oil to this mixture and while it is still warm add the yeast. Sift in the flour. Beat the eggs and add to the mixture.

3 Beat the mixture with an electric beater for about 1 minute. The mixture should be a thick batter. Add a little more warm water if too stiff. Fold the seeds into the mixture. Pour the batter into the prepared pan. Let it stand for 10–15 minutes or until mixture is puffy. It will continue to rise in the oven. Cook for about 20 minutes or until the loaves sound hollow when tapped.

Serves 2–4 • Preparation 25 minutes • Cooking 20 minutes

Bacon Bread Ring

1 teaspoon salt
1 teaspoon sugar
2 teaspoons psyllium
2 teaspoons gelatin
1 tablespoon dried yeast
1 egg white
½ teaspoon citric acid
¼ cup olive oil
250g/8 oz superfine flour (page 7)
125g/4 oz cooked bacon, crumbled

1 Grease a 3 x 8 in/8 x 20cm tube cake pan with margarine. Place the salt, sugar, psyllium and gelatin in 1 cup of cold water and let stand for 2 minutes. When the gelatin has softened, heat in a microwave for 10 seconds at a time, until dissolved.

2 Stir the yeast into the gelatin mixture and whisk slightly. Let stand for 10 minutes. Beat the egg white and citric acid until stiff, and add to yeast mixture with the oil and flour. Using an electric mixer beat well for about 2 minutes. Cover and let rise for 10 minutes. Whisk for 1 minute. Fold in the chopped bacon pieces.

3 Preheat the oven to 360°F/180°C. Spoon into the prepared baking pan, cover and let rise for 20 minutes. Place pan in the center of the oven and bake for 40 minutes. Remove from the oven and wrap in a clean tea towel to cool.

Serves 2 • Preparation 45 minutes • Cooking 40 minutes

Baps

1 teaspoon sugar
1 tablespoon gelatin
1 tablespoon dried yeast
2 egg whites
1 teaspoon salt
½ teaspoon citric acid
250g/8 oz superfine flour (page 7)
2 tablespoons olive oil

1 Grease a extra large muffin tin with some dairy-free margarine. Place the sugar and gelatin in 1 cup of cold water and let stand for 1 minute to soften, or until the liquid is clear. Add the yeast and stand for 10 minutes.

2 Whisk the eggs, salt and citric acid in a separate bowl with an electric mixer until stiff. Tip the flour into the yeast mixture. Beat in the oil and whisked eggs for 1 minute with electric mixer. Cover and let stand again for 10 minutes.

3 Preheat the oven to 360°F/180°C. Spoon the mixture into the cups and let rise until puffy – about 15 minutes. Dust the tops with sifted flour. Place in the center of the oven and bake for 10 minutes.

4 Remove from the oven and wrap in a clean kitchen towel to cool then place in a plastic bag until ready to serve.

Baps are simple bread rolls made with yeast. The outside is wonderfully crisp while the inside is soft, airy, and just waiting for a slab of butter.

Serves 2–4 • Preparation 35 minutes • Cooking 10 minutes

Black Bread

2 tablespoons poppy seeds
1 teaspoon salt
¼ cup molasses
1 tablespoon dried yeast
160g/6 oz superfine flour (page 7)
90g/3 oz sunflower meal
1 tablespoon carob
1 tablespoon psyllium
100g/3½ oz brown rice flour
1 egg
¼ cup olive oil
1 tablespoon caraway seeds

1   Grease an oven-proof bowl or round cake pan with margarine. Sprinkle the bottom with poppy seeds. Add the salt, molasses and yeast to 1 cup of warm water and stand 10 minutes.

2   Combine the flour, sunflower meal, carob, psyllium and rice flour. Add half the flour mixture to the yeast and whisk in the egg and oil then beat in the remaining flour with an electric mixer. Cover and let stand again for 15 minutes.

3   Preheat the oven to 360°F/180°C. Whisk the bread mixture, add the caraway seeds, pour into the prepared bowl or pan and let rise for about 20 minutes. Place in the middle of the oven and bake for about 40 minutes. Remove from the oven and cool in the tin. Wrap in a clean kitchen towel and refrigerate overnight before cutting.

This gluten-free version of traditional Hungarian black bread is hearty and delicious with sweet or savory toppings. You can make your own sunflower meal by blending sunflower seeds in the food processor for a minute or two.

Serves 2–4 • Preparation 1 hour 30 minutes • Cooking 40 minutes

Challah Ring

1 tablespoon gelatin
3 tablespoons sesame seeds
2 tablespoons dried yeast
3 egg whites
2 tablespoons sugar
2 teaspoons salt
1 teaspoon citric acid
500g/17½ oz superfine flour (page 7)
3 tablespoons olive oil

1 Grease a bundt pan with margarine and sprinkle with the sesame seeds. Place 2 cups of cold water into a large glass bowl or microwave dish. Add gelatin and let stand for 1 minute to soften. Heat the gelatin mixture for 50 seconds or until gelatin is dissolved.

2 Add the yeast and let stand for 10 minutes. Whisk the eggs, sugar, salt and citric acid in a separate bowl, with an electric mixer until stiff.

3 Tip the flour into the wet mixture. Beat in the oil and whisked eggs for 1 minute with electric mixer. Cover the bowl and let stand again for 10 minutes.

4 Preheat the oven to 400°F/200°C. Whisk again and pour the mixture into the pan and leave for about 20 minutes to rise. Place in the center of the oven and bake for 45 minutes. Remove from the oven and wrap in a clean kitchen towel to cool then place in a plastic bag until ready to serve.

Serves 2–4 • Preparation 40 minutes • Cooking 45 minutes

Irish Griddle Bread

½ cup milk, warmed
1 teaspoon sugar
2 tablespoons baby rice cereal
200g/7 oz superfine flour (page 7)
2 teaspoons gluten-free baking powder
2 tablespoons olive oil

1   Place the warm milk in a medium mixing bowl and add the sugar, baby rice cereal, three quarters of the flour and the baking powder. Mix well with a knife. Place the remaining flour on a board and tip the bread mix onto it. Knead lightly until all the flour is absorbed.

2   Oil the bowl the bread was mixed in with 1 tablespoon of olive oil. Place the dough back in the bowl and roll it around in the oiled basin to cover the surface with oil. Cover with a cloth and let rest for 10 minutes.

3   Remove dough from the bowl and flatten on a board to form a circle to fit the base of your pan. If too sticky use a little fine rice flour to press out the dough.

4   Oil a heavy frying pan and heat to a medium heat. Using the board to lift the dough, tip it into the pan. Adjust the size if necessary by pressing out a little more with your fingers. Cut the dough into four quarters with a knife. Cook the bread for 3 minutes on the medium heat before turning with a spatula. Reduce the pan heat to low and continue to cook for an additional 10 minutes until the bread sounds hollow when tapped.

Serves 1–2 • Preparation 25 minutes • Cooking 15 minutes

Herb Focaccia

1 teaspoon gelatin
pinch salt
1 teaspoon sugar
1 tablespoon dried yeast
¼ cup olive oil
140g/5 oz superfine flour (page 7)
1 egg or egg substitute
1 teaspoon mixed herbs
1 teaspoon sesame seeds

1 Grease the sides of a round bread pan and cut a circle of parchment paper to line the bottom. Add the gelatin, salt and sugar to ½ cup cold water and let stand for 1 minute. Heat the mix until the gelatin dissolves. Add the yeast and stand for 10 minutes.

2 Using an electric mixer beat in the oil, flour and egg for about 1 minute to make sure the yeast is well distributed. Stir in the mixed herbs.

3 Preheat the oven to 440°F/220°C. Pour the batter into one or two prepared pans and leave the mixture to stand for 20 minutes until bubbles form – it will not rise much in the pan.

4 Sprinkle the top with sesame seeds and cook for 10–20 minutes depending on thickness.

This delicious bread can be made in one or two round cake pans, depending on how thick you like it.

Serves 2 • Preparation 20 minutes • Cooking 20 minutes

Cheese Bread

1 teaspoon salt
130g/5 oz butter
250g/8 oz superfine flour (page 7)
5 eggs
250g/8 oz Gruyère cheese, cubed
30g/1 oz Cheddar cheese, grated

1 Preheat oven to 400°F/200°C. Cover a large baking sheet with silicone baking sheet. Place 1½ cups of water, salt and butter in a saucepan and bring to a boil. When boiling add all the flour and combine with a wooden spoon. Cook, stirring until mixture leaves the side of pan.

2 When cool add the eggs one at a time, stirring briskly with wooden spoon. Add the Gruyère cubes to the pastry and mix well.

3 Heap the mixture like a cake, onto the center of the baking sheet. Sprinkle with the grated cheddar cheese. Cook for 1 hour.

Serves 2–4 • Preparation 15 minutes • Cooking 60 minutes

Pumpernickel Bread

60g/2 oz fine polenta
1 teaspoon salt
¼ cup molasses
¼ cup olive oil
100g/3½ oz superfine flour (page 7)
60g/2 oz brown rice flour
1 tablespoon dried yeast
1 egg
1 tablespoon carob
1 tablespoon caraway seeds

1 Grease a small 7 x 4 x 4 in/18 x 11 x 10cm loaf pan with some margarine and line it with silicone coated parchment paper. Place 1½ cups of boiling water in a saucepan over high heat and slowly whisk the polenta into the rapidly boiling water. Cook for a few minutes until smooth. Add the salt, molasses and oil and leave to cool slightly.

2 Add half the flour, brown rice flour and the yeast to the warm mixture and let stand for 15 minutes. Whisk in the egg, remaining flour, and carob with an electric mixer. Stir in caraway seeds. Cover and let stand again for 15 minutes.

3 Preheat the oven to 300°F/150°C. Fill a large baking dish 9 x 13in/23 x 33cm halfway with hot water and place in the oven. Pour the mixture into the loaf pan and let rise for 30 minutes. Carefully place the loaf pan into the water bath and cook for 2 hours. Remove from oven and cool in the pan. Wrap in a clean kitchen towel and refrigerate overnight before slicing.

Serves 2–4 • Preparation 1 hour 10 minutes • Cooking 2 hours

Pocket Bread

1 teaspoon honey
1 teaspoon gelatin
2 teaspoons psyllium
1 teaspoon salt
1 tablespoon dried yeast
300g/10 oz superfine flour (page 7)

1 teaspoon paprika
½ teaspoon cayenne pepper
3 tablespoons olive oil
¼ cup fine rice flour for rolling

1 Place a heavy baking sheet in the oven and preheat to 360°F/180°C.

2 Cut 4 x 6 in/15cm circles of parchment paper. Place 200mL/7 oz of warm water in a bowl and add the honey, gelatin, psyllium, salt and yeast. Stir with a fork, cover and let stand for 5 minutes.

3 Add half the flour to the yeast mixture. Cover and stand to rise for 10 minutes. Add the remainder of the flour, spices and oil. Mix well with a knife using a cutting action and tip onto a board.

4 Knead for a few minutes until smooth, using the rice flour if necessary. Divide the dough into four balls. Press out half a ball on each paper, using your fingers with a little rice flour if necessary. Cover remaining dough with a cloth to prevent drying. Place circles on the baking sheet. Press out matching circles of dough, using oil to assist.

5 Brush halfway around the bottom circle with water to stick the top and leave an opening. Top the bottom dough portions with the 'lid' and peel back the oiled plastic to use again to make the next lid.

6 Cover the prepared pockets with a cloth and let stand about for 20 minutes. Brush with a little oil. Cook for 5 minutes in the preheated oven, then reduce the heat and cook for another 3 minutes. Remove from the oven and wrap in a cloth and place in a plastic bag to cool. Parchment paper circles can be reused next time.

This Persian pocket bread makes a great lunch, filled with salad. When making gluten-free pastry, putting fine rice flour in a shaker is very useful.

Serves 2 • Preparation 40 minutes • Cooking 10 minutes

Basic Bun Dough

1 tablespoon gelatin
1 tablespoon psyllium
2 tablespoons sugar
1 teaspoon salt
2 tablespoons glycerine
1 tablespoon dried yeast
450g/16 oz superfine flour (page 7)
1 egg
1 tablespoon pumpkin pie spice (optional)
2 tablespoons soft margarine

1 Place 7 oz/200mL of cold water in a microwave bowl and sprinkle the gelatin and psyllium on top. Let stand for a few minutes to soften and heat until gelatin dissolves.

2 Remove from heat, add sugar, salt, glycerine and yeast, and stir to mix. Cover and stand for 20 minutes until mixture is doubled. Oil a sheet of plastic about 12 x 9 in/30 x 22cm.

3 Using an electric mixer whisk about three-quarters of the flour into the yeast mixture. Add the egg, spice and margarine and beat until a smooth batter forms.

4 Cover and stand again for 20 minutes, then beat again for 1 minute. Using a spatula fold in the remaining flour and tip onto the plastic sheet. Lightly knead using a little fine rice flour if required. If you find it a little sticky when kneading, add a bit of fine rice flour. The dough should be as soft as possible to make a light textured bun.

5 Preheat oven to 360°F/180°C. Divide the dough into a lightly greased popover pan or large muffin tin. Let rise for 20 minutes and bake for 30 minutes until golden and puffed.

Preparation 50 minutes • Cooking as required

Lunch and Dinner

It is estimated that 1 out of 100 Americans has celiac disease. Only 3% have been diagnosed, but it's not surprising that so many people look for gluten-free recipes to feel better. It's even more challenging when cooking for a crowd with different dietary restrictions. We've pulled together our best recipes for pastas, pies—even pizza—that are tasty, tried, and true for the whole family.

Spring Rolls

2 teaspoons salt
2 teaspoons psyllium
200g/7 oz superfine flour (page 7)
3 tablespoons olive oil

Suggested Fillings
lightly cooked ground turkey, pork, beef, or shrimp
shredded cabbage, carrots, and bean sprouts
fresh cilantro

1 Place 1 cup of warm water, salt and psyllium in a bowl. Using a wire whisk add the flour and oil. Let stand for 5 minutes. If using a non-stick pan wipe it out with a paper towel and a small amount of oil to remove any particles that can cause the wraps to stick. If you are using a stainless steel pan, melt a little butter in the pan, then wipe it out with paper towel, then regrease it with a little more butter.

2 Heat the pan on medium heat. Pour about ¼ cup of batter (depending on the size of the pan) in the center of the pan. Lift the pan, and roll the mixture around to coat the bottom of the pan with a thin layer. Let cook for 1 minute, until it will slide out of the pan. You don't want a lot of color on the wraps. Place the wrap onto a clean kitchen towel and cover to prevent drying. Continue with the rest of the batter. When cool, store wraps in a plastic bag in the refrigerator until you are ready to use them.

3 To cook the spring rolls, lay the wraps flat and spoon filling onto the center. Brush the edges with a little egg white, fold in the ends, parcel style, and roll up to seal. Deep fry in hot oil for a few minutes until golden.

You can make spring rolls in advance and freeze in aluminum foil. Defrost at room temperature before using.

Serves 2 • Preparation 20 minutes • Cooking 10 minutes

Fried Mushrooms

1 egg
1 teaspoon gluten-free baking powder
100g/3½ oz Lola's bread and pastry flour (page 7)
1 teaspoon freshly ground black pepper
1 teaspoon salt
250g/8 oz fresh button mushrooms
2 cups olive oil for frying

1 Whisk together the egg and ¼ cup of cold water. Toss in the flour, baking powder, salt and pepper. Whisk the mixture until it forms a smooth batter. Let stand for 5 minutes.

2 Heat the olive oil in a deep saucepan. Dip each mushroom into the batter. Using tongs or a fork, lower the mushrooms, one at a time, into the hot oil. Cook until pale golden, turning if necessary and when cooked drain on paper towel.

Serve with green salad and sour cream for a delicious entrée.

Serves 1 • Preparation 15 minutes • Cooking 12 minutes

Gnocchi

500g/1 lb russet potatoes
2 tablespoons gelatin or agar powder
1 teaspoon psyllium
2 egg yolks
pinch of nutmeg
1 teaspoon salt
¾ cup superfine flour (page 7)

1 Boil the potatoes with their skins on. Cool, peel and grate the potato.

2 Place the gelatin or agar, psyllium and egg yolks in 2 tablespoons warm water and whisk slightly to mix, then add nutmeg and salt. Let stand 5 minutes. Mix the shredded potato into the mixture and add enough flour to form a soft dough (about ½ cup). Roll into balls using the extra flour, then make a depression with your thumb in each. Set in the refrigerator for at least an hour before cooking.

3 Roll out in a sausage shape, then cut into 30 small pieces. Place the gnocchi in a pot of boiling water and cook for about 10 minutes, until they float. Remove with a draining spoon and serve with your favorite sauce.

Serves 2 • Preparation 35 minutes • Cooking 25 minutes

Spinach Fettuccine

½ cup spinach, blanched
1 tablespoon psyllium
1 teaspoon gelatin
3 eggs
1 tablespoon olive oil
300g/10½ oz superfine flour (page 7) plus 55g/2 oz extra for rolling

1 Place ¼ cup water in a bowl and using a blender, process the spinach into the water until there are no visible pieces and you have a green liquid. Add the psyllium and gelatin and let stand for 5 minutes.

2 Add the eggs and oil to a food processor with the softened psyllium and gelatin mix. Blend in 300g/10½ oz of the flour. Turn onto a lightly oiled plastic sheet and knead in the remaining flour. Cover and rest for 1 hour.

3 Divide mixture into four. Start rolling one part, keeping the other pieces moist in a plastic bag.

4 Using a pasta machine, Roll the pasta through the machine on the largest setting. Fold into thirds, lightly flour the pasta and roll again. Repeat this process several times, lowering the machine setting to roll the pasta thinner before rolling through the machine cutter.

5 Wrap the fettuccine loosely around your fingers to form a nest, then refrigerate in a single layer in an airtight container or dry on a kitchen towel overnight. The pasta can be stored for about 2 weeks in an airtight container when dry.

6 Bring a pot of heavily salted water to a boil. Add the pasta and cook for about 5 minutes. Do not stir. Turn off the heat and let the pasta cook until tender. Carefully lift the pasta with a scoop and top with your favorite sauce, such as pesto, browned butter and cheese, or fresh tomato basil sauce.

Serves 2 • Preparation 35 minutes • Cooking 20 minutes

Beef Soup with Dumplings

500g/1 lb stew meat, cut into 3cm cubes
3 large potatoes, cut into 3cm cubes
3 large onions, coarsely chopped
2 large carrots, cut crosswise into 2cm rounds
400g/14 oz canned tomatoes
1 large turnip, coarsely diced
2 celery stalks, coarsely chopped
2 or 3 sauce blocks (page 9)
2 cups spinach leaves, shredded
400g/14 oz canned kidney beans, drained
salt and freshly ground black pepper

Dumplings
1 tablespoon psyllium
1 egg
1 tablespoon olive oil
100g/10½ oz Lola's bread and pastry flour (page 7)
2 teaspoon gluten-free baking powder
½ teaspoon salt

1 Combine the meat, potatoes, onions, carrots, tomatoes, turnip and celery in a large saucepan. Cover with cold water and simmer for 1 hour.

2 To make the dumplings, sprinkle the psyllium on 2 tablespoons cold water and leave for a few minutes to gel. Whisk the egg and combine with the oil, flour, baking powder, salt and then the psyllium mix.

3 Use a tablespoon to form 2–3 in/6–8cm round dumplings and add to the boiling soup for 1 hour. Remove and test the dumplings – if they are still doughy cook for another 15 minutes and test again. When done, remove the dumplings and thicken the soup with one or two sauce blocks to your desired consistency, stir in the spinach leaves and the beans and season with salt and pepper. Serve with dumplings.

Serves 4 • Preparation 35 minutes • Cooking 2 hours

Seafood Linguine

Gluten-Free Linguine
1 tablespoon psyllium husks
1 teaspoon gelatin
3 eggs
1 tablespoon olive oil
300g/10½ oz Lola's bread and pastry flour
  (page 7)

Seafood Sauce
4 mussels in shell

2 filets white fish, approximately
  200g/7 oz, cut into pieces
125g/4 oz shrimp
125g/4 oz scallops
3 sauce blocks (page 9)
small bunch green onions, chopped
1 stalk celery, diced
salt and paprika to taste
few sprigs dill

1 To make the pasta, place ¼ cup of water in a bowl and add the psyllium and gelatin.
   Add the eggs and oil to a food processor with the softened psyllium and gelatin mix.
   Blend in 300g/10½ oz of the flour. Turn onto a lightly oiled plastic sheet and knead in
   the remaining flour. Cover and rest for 1 hour. Divide the mixture into four; start rolling
   one part, keeping the other pieces moist in a plastic bag.

2 Using a pasta machine, process the pastry by rolling through the machine. Fold into
   three, lightly flour the underside and roll again, making sure that the folded edges are
   at the side of the machine to give a neat edge. Repeat the process six times before
   making shapes. Dry the finished pasta on a clean kitchen towel overnight to store
   for a few weeks or keep in the refrigerator to cook in the next few days. Use plenty
   of heavily salted water to cook the pasta. Bring to a boil, add the pasta and cook for
   about 5 minutes. Do not stir. Turn off the heat and leave to stand until the pasta is
   tender. Lift the pasta carefully from the water with a pasta scoop and place in a large
   serving dish. Scrub the mussel shells and toss them for a few minutes in a pan to open.

3 To make the sauce, place the white fish, shrimp and scallops in a saucepan with
   2 cups of cold water and bring to simmer. Turn off the heat and let stand for a few
   minutes to finish cooking. Remove the seafood and set aside. Add the sauce blocks
   to the hot fish stock and, when melted, return the mixture to the heat and stir until
   thickened; stir in the vegetables and add seasoning and some dill if desired. Combine
   the fish, scallops, shrimp and mussels with the sauce and pour over the pasta. When
   ready to serve, cover the dish and warm for a few minutes in the oven.

Serves 4 • Preparation 35 minutes • Cooking 30 minutes

Basic Pie Crust

2 tablespoons gelatin
½ cup olive oil
300g/10½ oz Lola's bread and pastry flour (page 7)
1 teaspoon baking soda
1 teaspoon salt
juice of ½ lemon

1 Sprinkle the gelatin on ½ cup of cold water and let soften. Place the gelatin mixture and oil in a large saucepan and heat to dissolve the gelatin. Remove the oil mixture from the heat and sift in the dry ingredients. Add enough lemon juice to form a soft dough.

2 Mix the dough until it forms a ball and will leave the sides of the saucepan. Tip out on to plastic wrap and knead through the wrap, lifting and turning until the pastry is smooth. Allow to cool slightly before use. Roll out between two sheets of wrap using a small amount of oil on your hands if necessary.

This pastry is free of dairy products, gluten, wheat, soy and sugar. There is no sugar in this recipe making it perfect for diabetics. In most cases the sweetener can be added to the filling, but if you wish you can add 2 tablespoons of powdered sugar to the flour. This will make the pastry a little 'sticky' but is good for a pie crust that requires little handling. The pastry does not shrink so can be used for blind-baked goods such as tarts.

Serves 2 • Preparation 20 minutes • Cooking 5 minutes

Chicken Pizza

1 teaspoon salt
1 teaspoon sugar
1 teaspoon agar powder
3 teaspoons dried yeast
150g/5 oz Lola's bread and pastry flour (page 7)

Toppings
200g/7 oz boneless, skinless chicken breast
1 red onion, sliced into rings
4 sprigs oregano, leaves removed and finely chopped
12 oven-dried tomatoes
3 tablespoons dairy-free margarine
1 cup rice crumbs
1 teaspoon paprika

1 Preheat the oven to 430°F/220°C. Grease a 12 in/30cm pizza pan with margarine. Place the salt, sugar, agar and yeast in ¾ cup warm water, whisk slightly and stand for 10 minutes. Stir in the flour and whisk well and stand for another 10 minutes.

2 Pour the batter onto the greased pan, and spread with a spatula, creating a thin, even layer. Let the mixture stand for 10 minutes while cooking the chicken.

3 Cut the chicken into long strips. Lightly brown one side of the chicken in a hot pan, then add some water to the pan, and turn the chicken over. Don't overcook the chicken, as it is going to be cooked again in the oven.

4 Arrange onions, herbs, and chicken, and tomatoes on the dough. Melt the margarine. Stir in rice crumbs and paprika. Mix well and sprinkle over the pizza. Bake for 20–25 minutes.

Serves 2 • Preparation 20 minutes • Cooking 50 minutes

Moussaka

2 large or 4 small eggplant
salt and freshly ground black pepper
500g/1 lb ground lamb
2 cloves garlic, minced
2 onions, finely chopped
¼ cup olive oil
400g/14 oz canned tomatoes
½ bunch oregano, leaves picked and
  chopped

½ cup basil, chopped
½ bunch thyme, leaves picked
½ cup parsley, chopped
2 cups milk
3 sauce blocks (page 9)
3 eggs, lightly whisked
60g/2 oz mozzarella cheese, grated

1 Slice the eggplant in thick slices, sprinkle with salt and set aside. Combine the lamb, garlic, onion, salt and pepper.

2 Use 1 tablespoon of the oil to grease a heavy pan. Brown the meat without stirring – until it smells like barbecued lamb, turn once and brown again for a few minutes. Add the tomatoes, herbs and ½ a cup of cold water. Place in a saucepan and simmer for 15 minutes.

3 Rinse the salt from the eggplant with cold water and dry with paper towel. Place the remainder of the oil in a large frying pan and sauté the eggplant for 5 minutes on each side. Drain on paper towel.

4 Preheat the oven to 320°F/160°C. Heat the milk in a saucepan until boiling, add the sauce blocks and whisk to form a thin sauce. Add the eggs to the custard. Use a large ovenproof casserole dish to bake your moussaka. Pour a thin layer of custard in the bottom of the dish. Arrange a layer of eggplant slices on the custard, then a thick layer of the lamb mixture. Continue to layer the eggplant and meat until it is all used. Pour the custard over the casserole and finish with the mozzarella cheese.

5 Bake for 1 hour, then turn the heat off and leave in the oven until set (about another half hour). Serve with a green salad.

Sauce blocks used in this recipe will prevent the mixture curdling and give a firm texture when serving.

Serves 4 • Preparation 35 minutes • Cooking 95 minutes

Spanish Rice with Seafood

250g/8 oz white boneless fish
125g/4 oz shrimp
3–4 sauce blocks (page 9)
salt and freshly ground black pepper
2 stalks celery, diced
1 large onion, diced

Spanish Rice Topping
1 cup rice
400g/14 oz canned peeled tomatoes
1 tablespoon sugar
1 tablespoon gluten-free curry powder
2 tablespoons melted margarine
¼ cup rice crumbs

1 Place the fish and shrimp in a large saucepan and cover with cold water, bring to a boil and simmer for 5 minutes. Strain the fish and retain the stock to make the sauce.

2 Thicken the stock with the sauce blocks to make a thick sauce. Season, add the celery, onion, fish and shrimp to the sauce. Spoon the fish into a casserole dish.

3 To make the topping, place the rice in a large microwave bowl with the cold water. Microwave on high for 10 minutes and let stand for 10 minutes until the rice is tender and the water has evaporated. Stir with a fork to separate.

4 Mash the canned tomatoes and reduce by cooking over a low heat with the sugar and curry powder for about 15 minutes. Add this mixture to the cooked rice and stir to combine. Pile on top of the seafood mixture. Top with 2 tablespoons melted margarine combined with ¼ cup rice crumbs.

Serves 2 • Preparation 25 minutes • Cooking 35 minutes

Seafood Chowder in Bread Bowls

Bread Bowls
1 teaspoon sesame seeds
1 medium potato, peeled and cut into
  2mm cubes
¼ cup olive oil
1 tablespoon gelatin
1 teaspoon sugar
1 teaspoon salt
1 tablespoon dried yeast
240g/8 oz superfine flour (page 7)
30g/1 oz baby rice flake cereal
1 egg

Seafood Chowder
250g/8 oz filet white fish, sliced
150g/5 oz scallops
125g/4 oz shrimp
60g/2 oz butter
100g/10½ oz superfine flour (page 7)
½ cup white wine
1 teaspoon red pepper flakes
salt and freshly ground black pepper
1 cup cooked potato, sliced
½ cup chopped celery
½ cup chopped onion

1 To make the bread bowls, preheat oven to 400°F/200°C, grease a large six-cup
   muffin tin and line with sesame seeds. Cook the potato in boiling water for
   10 minutes and mash with the olive oil. Place the gelatin in 200mL/7 oz of cold
   water and let stand to soften and then heat mixture until clear. Tip the hot gelatin
   mixture into the warm potato and mix well. Add, sugar and salt to this mixture
   and while it is still warm add the yeast. Stand for 5 minutes. Add the remaining
   ingredients and beat for 2 minutes with an electric mixer. Pour the batter into the
   prepared tins and let stand for 10–15 minutes. Cook for about 20 minutes or until
   they are firm and keep warm.

2 Meanwhile, simmer the fish, scallops and shrimp in 3 cups of water until lightly
   cooked. Strain the seafood and return the liquid to a boil. Add the vegetables and
   simmer for 10 minutes. Strain and reserve the liquid as stock. Melt butter in a
   saucepan and stir in the flour. Cook for 1 minute on a low heat. Add the stock and
   wine to the saucepan. Stir the sauce over a low heat until slightly thickened. Add
   the seasonings, vegetables and seafood.

3 Cut a lid off the buns, remove half of the bread filling and fill with the chowder.
   Serve immediately.

Serves 4 • Preparation 50 minutes • Cooking 1 hour

Quiche Lorraine

Crust
80g/3 oz butter
160g/6 oz Lola's bread and pastry flour (page 7)
1 tablespoon psyllium
1 teaspoon lemon juice

Filling
2 large slices lean bacon, chopped
60g/2 oz Cheddar cheese, grated
4 eggs
1 cup milk
salt and freshly ground black pepper
½ cup basic sauce (page 40)

1 Blend the crust ingredients together, adding a little water if necessary to form a soft dough and press into the quiche dish. Chill in the refrigerator for a 30 minutes before adding the filling.

2 Sprinkle the chopped bacon and cheese over the base of the crust. Lightly whisk the eggs and milk with the salt and pepper, add the basic sauce and pour over the cheese and bacon (basic sauce here prevents the quiche from curdling if your oven is too hot). Place the quiche onto a flat tray and freeze for at least an hour or until required. This can be done a day before if necessary.

3 Preheat oven to 320°F/160°C. Place the frozen quiche in the oven for 25 minutes or until firm to touch on the outside of the top. Turn the heat off and let cook for a few more minutes until the center is set – it is important not to overcook the filling. Serve hot.

For a dairy-free quiche, replace the milk with an additional cup of basic sauce (page 40). Cheese can be replaced by corn niblets and the crust made with the basic pie crust recipe (page 130).

Serves 4 • Preparation 35 minutes • Cooking 30 minutes

Curried Chicken Pies

1 green apple, chopped
1 onion, finely chopped
1 tablespoon olive oil
1 tablespoon gluten-free curry powder
1 tablespoon brown sugar
salt and freshly ground black pepper
500g/1 lb chicken breast, cut into 3cm
  cubes
1 tablespoon potato flour

1 cup coconut milk
2 sauce blocks (page 9)
1 small carrot, diced
1 stalk celery, chopped
300g/10½ oz basic pie crust
  (page 130)

1 Place the apple and onion in a hot pan with the oil. Add the curry powder, brown sugar, salt and pepper, stir over a moderate heat for a few minutes.

2 Toss the chicken pieces into a plastic bag with the potato flour and shake the bag to coat the meat with flour. Add the chicken meat to the curry mixture and stir-fry for a few minutes.

3 Add the coconut milk and bring the mixture to a boil, stirring to prevent burning. Remove from the heat, add the sauce blocks and let stand for a few minutes until the blocks have softened. Return to the heat and stir until the mixture is thick. Add the carrot and celery and simmer for 15 minutes, until the chicken meat is tender.

4 Preheat oven to 360°F/180°C. Roll out half the pastry between two sheets of plastic wrap and press into 5 in/12cm pie tins, leaving enough pastry to form the edge of the pie. Roll out the top of the pies and cut slits in the top to allow steam to escape. Pour the thickened pie meat into the uncooked pastry case.

5 Using a spatula, dip the lid of the pie into a plate of cold water and slide it onto the meat to form the top of the pie. Press with a fork to seal the edges of the pie. Glaze with egg wash or milk. Place in the oven and cook for about 25 minutes or until the base of the pie is crisp and firm to touch.

Makes 4 • Preparation 40 minutes • Cooking 60 minutes

Crab Tartlets

200g/7 oz canned crab meat

Pastry
2 teaspoons gelatin
125g/4 oz butter
250g/8 oz Lola's bread and pastry flour (page 7)

Custard
2 sauce blocks (page 9)
4 eggs, lightly whisked
1 cup milk
salt and freshly ground black pepper
¼ bunch chives, chopped
paprika for garnish

1 Preheat oven to 320°F/160°C. Grease mini-muffin tin. Sprinkle the gelatin on 3 tablespoons of cold water and leave to stand for a few minutes. Chop the butter into blocks and combine all the pastry ingredients to form a firm dough, kneading either, by hand or in a food processor. Cover the pastry while you mix the filling.

2 To make the custard, add the sauce blocks to a cup of boiling water and when they have melted whisk well. Add the eggs, milk, salt, pepper and chives. Pour into a pitcher for easy pouring into muffin cups.

3 Divide pastry into four pieces for ease of handling. Roll the pastry between two sheets of plastic wrap and cut circles using a small glass or cookie cutter to fit into muffin cups. Press each circle firmly into the bottom of each cup, place a small amount of crab meat in each cup and top with custard. Sprinkle with paprika. Freeze until ready to cook, or for at least 1 hour. Cook for 30 minutes, or until the custard is set. Serve hot.

Makes 24 • Preparation 30 minutes + freezing time • Cooking 40 minutes

Desserts

No need to hide in a corner when the dessert is dished out. Lola has developed a fantastic series of recipes – all gluten free, to really trap the taste buds. You will enjoy such treats as Apple and Rhubarb Crumble and Fruit Flans together with a whole host of tasty delights.

Fairy Cakes

4 eggs
200g/7 oz sugar
200g/7 oz Lola's all-purpose flour (page 7)
60g/2 oz ground almonds
1 tablespoon vanilla extract
2 tablespoons psyllium
2 tablespoons gelatin
3 teaspoons gluten-free baking powder
200g/7 oz butter or margarine

1 Preheat the oven to 360°F/180°C. Line 24 muffin tins with cupcake liners. Do not bake without the paper liners—cakes will stick. Don't use aluminium tins.

2 Combine all ingredients in a large bowl and mix for 1 minute. Spoon into cupcake liners and let rest for 5 minutes.

3 Bake on the top rack of the oven until just firm to the touch, about 10 minutes. Frost or decorate as desired.

4 Cakes will retain their moisture for several days kept in a cake tin and will freeze well in foil or a plastic container.

These yummy cupcakes are delicious frosted with with colored lemon or orange icing (see pages 56 and 60 for recipes). They freeze well and will keep for several days in a plastic air-tight container or foil, but not a plastic bag.

Makes 24 cakes • Preparation 20 minutes • Cooking 10 minutes

Rum Balls

60g/2 oz dairy-free margarine
2 tablespoons molasses
60g/2 oz brown sugar
1 tablespoon cocoa
1 tablespoon rum
2 tablespoons almond meal
1 cup mixed chopped raisins and prunes
1 cup chopped mixed nuts: flaked almonds, cashews, walnuts and hazelnuts

1 Place the margarine, molasses and brown sugar in a saucepan and slowly bring
   to a boil.
2 Remove from the heat and stir in the remaining ingredients. Mix well by hand
   or in a food processor. Cool and roll into balls. Coat as desired.

**These beautiful and decadent rum balls can be rolled in melted chocolate, cocoa,
shredded coconut or finely chopped nuts. Set out a variety of toppings in small
bowls before rolling out the dough, so you can drop them directly into your topping
of choice, roll them around, then set on a serving plate.**

Serves 2–4 • Preparation 10 minutes • Cooking 10 minutes

Lamingtons

1 teaspoon butter
100g/3½ oz sugar
1 teaspoon vanilla extract
100g/3½ oz Lola's all-purpose flour (page 7)
1 teaspoon gluten-free baking powder
3 large eggs

Chocolate Icing
200g/7 oz powdered sugar
1 tablespoon cocoa
1 teaspoon butter
150g/5 oz shredded coconut
1 teaspoon vanilla extract

1 Preheat the oven to 320°F/160°C. Grease an 8 in/20cm square pan and line the bottom of the pan with parchment paper. Place the butter in a small bowl, add the vanilla and 3 teaspoons of hot water, and let stand for 1 minute.

2 Place the eggs and sugar in a metal bowl and whisk with a wire whisk over a saucepan of hot water until the mixture is warm and slightly frothy. Remove from the heat and continue beating with a rotary or electric beater until the mixture is thick and creamy but not stiff.

3 Carefully sift the flour and baking powder into the egg mixture. Pour the warm butter mix around the sides of the bowl as you continue to fold the mixture. Quickly pour into the prepared cake tin and place in the center of the oven.

4 Cook for 15 minutes. Let stand in the oven for an extra 5 minutes with the door ajar. Cool the cake and cut into squares. Freeze the squares for about 20 minutes.

5 Make icing by sifting the cocoa and powdered sugar together into a large bowl. Dissolve the butter in a little hot water, add to the cocoa and sugar, and stir until smooth. Coat each frozen cake square with icing and roll in shredded coconut.

Lamingtons are chocolate sponge cake cut into squares and coated in chocolate icing and coconut. They freeze beautifully.

Serves 4–6 • Preparation 40 minutes • Cooking 20 minutes

Date Bars

Pastry
1 tablespoon gelatin
1 egg
125g/4 oz butter
2 tablespoons powdered sugar
300g/10 oz Lola's all-purpose flour
  (page 7)

Filing
200g/7 oz dates
1 tablespoon brown sugar

1 tablespoon water
½ tablespoon honey
½ tablespoon light corn syrup
1 teaspoon pumpkin pie spice

Lemon Icing
125g/4 oz sifted pure icing sugar
1 teaspoon melted butter
lemon juice

1 Preheat the oven to 360°F/180°C. Soak the gelatin in ¼ cup cold water, then heat gently until dissolved. Cool. Combine all the remaining pastry ingredients in a food processor and process to form a firm pastry.

2 Divide the pastry and press half of the mixture into an ungreased 8 in/20cm square pan. Use fingers to form a crust. Roll out the remaining half of the pastry between two sheets of plastic wrap and set aside.

3 Warm the dates slightly over a saucepan of hot water. Combine the remainder of the filling ingredients with the softened dates in a food processor and process into a coarse paste.

4 Spread the filling onto the bottom crust and cover with the rolled sheet of pastry. Prick the top with tines of fork to allow air to escape and crust to cook evenly. Brush with water and sprinkle with sugar. Bake for 20 minutes and allow to cool in the pan.

5 Make the lemon icing by combining powdered sugar, melted butter and 1 tablespoon of hot water. Add lemon juice until smooth and thin enough to pour over the date bars. Cut into squares.

Serves 2–4 • Preparation 40 minutes • Cooking 20 minutes

Almond Cookies

100g/3½ oz Lola's all-purpose flour (page 7)
100g/3½ oz sugar
1 teaspoon baking soda
45g/1½ oz slivered almonds
30g/1 oz ground almonds
30g/1 oz baby rice cereal
⅓ cup olive oil
1 tablespoon water
3 tablespoons liquid glucose
3 teaspoons vanilla extract
1 teaspoon almond extract

1 Preheat the oven to 320°F/160°C. Line a baking sheet with parchment paper or foil. In a large bowl, combine flour, sugar, baking soda, slivered almonds, ground almonds, and rice cereal. Mix well.

2 Place the oil, water and glucose into a large saucepan and heat slowly to a simmer. Remove the saucepan from the heat and add the dry ingredients to the oil mixture. Add the vanilla and almond extracts and mix well.

3 Turn dough onto a large sheet of plastic wrap and roll into a long thin tube. Slice into 16 slices and place onto prepared baking sheet. Cook for 10–15 minutes or until pale golden brown. Cool on the tray.

These cookies are great for making ahead of time. Simply wrap the log of dough in plastic wrap and refrigerate until ready to use. Let the dough come to room temperature before slicing.

Makes 16 cookies • Preparation 25 minutes • Cooking 15 minutes

Cinnamon Squares

90g/3 oz dairy-free margarine
2 teaspoons vanilla extract
150g/5 oz Lola's all-purpose flour (page 7)
150g/5 oz sugar
1 tablespoon ground cinnamon
2 egg yolks
2 tablespoons fine rice flour
2 tablespoons olive oil

1 Preheat the oven to 300°F/150°C. Line a baking sheet with parchment paper.
2 Place all the ingredients except the rice flour and oil in a mixer and blend for a few minutes until the mixture forms a ball. Tip onto a sheet of plastic wrap.
3 Knead a few times with the rice flour, then roll out into a thick slab. Cut into squares using knife or cookie cutter.
4 Place on the prepared tray. Brush with olive oil and bake for 10 minutes. Sprinkle with mixture of 3 parts sugar to 1 part cinnamon and let cool on the baking sheet.

Serves 2–4 • Preparation 12 minutes • Cooking 10 minutes

Ginger Madelines

1 tablespoon egg substitute
3 tablespoons olive oil
¼ cup pear nectar or rice syrup
1 tablespoon vanilla extract
150g/5 oz Lola's all-purpose flour (page 7)
1 tablespoon ground ginger
½ teaspoon salt
2 teaspoons gluten-free baking powder
100g/3½ oz xylityol

1 Preheat the oven to 320°F/160°C. Lightly grease 12 madeline molds with dairy-free margarine. Place ½ cup warm water in a mixing bowl, add egg substitute and let stand for about 2 minutes.

2 Place the oil in a saucepan with the pear nectar or rice syrup and warm gently, then add the vanilla and remove from the heat.

3 Combine the flour, ginger, salt and baking powder in a separate bowl. Beat the warm water and egg substitute until creamy, then gradually add the xylitol and beat for a few minutes to form a meringue. Add the oil mix, then fold in the dry ingredients.

4 Spoon the mixture into the prepared tray and bake for 10–15 minutes or until firm to the touch.

Serves 4 • Preparation 15 minutes • Cooking 15 minutes

Tiny Teddies

1 tablespoon amaranth cereal
150g/5 oz Lola's all-purpose flour (page 7)
1 teaspoon baking soda
1 tablespoon cocoa powder
1 teaspoon ground ginger
¼ cup olive oil
¼ cup rice syrup
2 tablespoons extra-fine rice flour
1 tablespoon vanilla extract

1 Preheat the oven to 300°F/150°C. Line a baking sheet with parchment paper. Combine all the dry ingredients except the rice flour and mix well. In a saucepan on a gentle heat slowly bring the oil and syrup to boiling point.

2 Remove from heat and tip in the dry ingredients, then the vanilla. Using a wooden spoon mix until combined and tip onto a sheet of plastic wrap.

3 Knead a few times, using the rice flour if necessary. Roll out in a thick sheet and cut with a tiny teddy cutter.

4 Place on the prepared pan. Bake for 15 minutes and cool on the tray.

Serves 4 • Preparation 20 minutes • Cooking 15 minutes

Cinnamon Spice Stars

¼ cup olive oil
2 tablespoons molasses
300g/10 oz Lola's bread and pastry flour (page 7)
100g/3½ oz sugar
2 tablespoons ground ginger
1 tablespoon pumpkin pie spice
1 egg, lightly beaten
white icing or melted white chocolate

1 Preheat the oven to 300°F/150°C. Line a baking sheet with parchment paper. Gently heat oil and molasses in a saucepan until warm. Remove from heat and add ¾ of the flour, plus sugar, spices and egg. Mix well with wooden spoon.

2 Tip dough onto a sheet of plastic wrap and knead the remaining flour into the dough. Cover with another sheet of plastic and roll into a thin sheet. Cut into desired shapes and place on prepared baking sheet.

3 Bake on the middle rack of the oven for 10 minutes, or until firm to the touch. Cool on the tray.

Serves 2–4 • Preparation 20 minutes • Cooking 10 minutes

Fresh Fruit Flans

Crust
½ cup olive oil
2 tablespoons liquid glucose or rice syrup
100g/3½ oz Lola's bread and pastry flour
(page 7)
1 tablespoon baby rice cereal

Pastry Cream
60g/2 oz butter
3 tablespoons Lola's bread and pastry
flour (page 7)
1 teaspoon almond extract
2 teaspoons vanilla extract
60g/2 oz sugar

1 egg
1 cup milk
½ cup heavy cream

Topping
1 small can apricot halves
½ cup apricot syrup
150g/5 oz strawberries
3 kiwi fruit, sliced

Fruit Glaze
1 tablespoon gelatin
½ cup fruit syrup

1 To make the crust, preheat the oven to 320°F/160°C. Warm the olive oil and glucose and stir in the flour and rice cereal. Tip onto a sheet of plastic wrap and knead lightly. Let cool. Roll out between two sheets of plastic to fit six mini tart pans or one 8 in/20cm tart pan. Bake for 15–20 minutes.

2 To make the pastry cream, cream the butter, flour, extracts, sugar and egg together. Heat the milk on a low heat to near boiling, but do not boil. Tip the hot milk into the creamy mixture and whisk well to combine the ingredients. Return the mixture to the heat and cook for a few minutes until thickened. Remove the custard from the saucepan and set aside to cool. Whip the cream and fold into the cooled custard.

3 To make the fruit glaze, sprinkle gelatin on fruit syrup and let stand until the gelatin is soft. Place the mixture in a bowl over boiling water until the gelatin syrup is clear.

4 Fill the cooled pastry shells with pastry cream, piling it high to support the fruit. Arrange the fruit over the pastry cream and glaze it with a pastry brush and warm glaze.

Serves 4 • Preparation 30 minutes • Cooking 15 minutes

Pear Fritters with Low Sugar Caramel Sauce

1 tablespoon egg substitute
1 teaspoon gelatin or agar powder
2 tablespoons xylitol
1 teaspoon vanilla extract
100g/3½ oz superfine flour (page 7)
1 teaspoon gluten-free baking powder
2 cups olive oil
1 large pear, cored and cut crosswise into
  thick slices
cinnamon

Low-sugar caramel sauce
2 sauce blocks (page 9)
150g/5 oz dairy-free margarine
½ cup rice syrup
2 teaspoons caramel extract

1 To make the sauce, place 1 cup boiling water in a saucepan and add the sauce blocks. When the blocks have melted, stir over a low heat until you have a thickened sauce, then set aside to cool.

2 Melt the margarine in a saucepan over low heat, stir in the rice syrup and cook for about 2 minutes until the mixture turns a golden caramel color. Add the sauce to the margarine mixture and stir in the caramel extract. Beat well until smooth and creamy. Keep warm while you make the fritters.

3 To make the fritters, beat the egg substitute, gelatin or agar and ⅔ cup warm water with an electric beater until thick and frothy. Add the xylitol a little at a time and continue beating for an additional minute. Stir in the vanilla, flour and baking powder. Whisk well until the mixture is a smooth batter.

4 Heat the oil in a deep pan. Thinly coat the fruit with batter – if the batter is too thick, add a little more warm water. Gently lower the coated fruit into the hot oil. Turn once while cooking and cook until golden. Remove from the oil and drain on paper towel. Sprinkle with cinnamon and extra xylitol and serve warm with the caramel sauce.

Serves 4 • Preparation 30 minutes • Cooking 10 minutes

Baked Rice Pudding

2 tablespoons dairy-free margarine
2 tablespoons superfine flour (page 7)
1 cup rice milk
2 tablespoons sugar
1 teaspoon vanilla extract
½ cup cooked rice
1 tablespoon brown sugar
cinnamon

1 Melt the margarine and stir in the flour – cook for a few minutes until the mixture
   slides in the saucepan.
2 Add the rice milk and whisk well over the heat to produce a thick custard. Add the
   sugar, vanilla and cooked rice.
3 Spoon the mixture into ovenproof serving dishes and sprinkle with brown sugar
   and a little cinnamon. Broil for 5 minutes to brown the topping.

Serves 2 • Preparation 10 minutes • Cooking 8 minutes

Lemon Meringue Pie

125g/4 oz Lola's bread and pastry flour (page 7)
60g/2 oz dairy-free margarine
1 egg yolk
1 tablespoon rice syrup

Lemon Filling
60g/2 oz sugar
juice of 2 lemons
zest of 1 lemon
2 tablespoons tapioca starch
2 egg yolks

Meringue
3 egg whites
100g/3½ oz sugar

1 Preheat the oven to 360°F/160°C. Place the flour, margarine, egg yolk, rice syrup and 2 tablespoons cold water to mix in a food processor. Process until it forms a ball. Tip out and knead lightly, then press the crust into an ungreased 8 in/20cm tart pan with a removable base. Bake the crust for about 20 minutes. Set aside until cool.

2 Place 1 cup water, the sugar, lemon juice and zest in a saucepan, heat until near boiling point, then remove from heat. Mix the tapioca starch with 2 teaspoons cold water and stir into the juice mixture.

3 Return to the heat and stir until the mixture thickens. Whisk the yolks and add them to the mixture, stir well for about 1 minute over the heat.

4 Pour the lemon filling into the cooked crust. Beat the egg whites until they are stiff, then gradually add the sugar, beating until it has completely dissolved. Spoon on top of the lemon filling and bake for about 15 minutes.

Serves 4 • Preparation 25 minutes • Cooking 35 minutes

Apple Rhubarb Crisp

3 large baking apples, such as Jonathan, Braeburn, Gala or Granny Smith
½ cup sugar or sugar substitute
small bunch rhubarb, sliced crosswise

Topping
60g/2 oz butter
100g/3½ oz Lola's all-purpose flour (page 7)
100g/3½ oz sugar
100g/3½ oz almond meal

1 Preheat the oven to 400°F/200°C. Place the apples in a greased pie plate.
   Sprinkle with ½ cup sugar or substitute.
2 Cook the rhubarb gently for 10 minutes with 1 tablespoon sugar or to taste in
   a saucepan.
3 To make the topping, combine the topping ingredients together.
4 Tip the cooked juicy rhubarb over the raw apple and sprinkle with the topping.
   Bake for 20 minutes.

**This dessert can be made with canned or fresh apple, but the rhubarb needs to be
cooked separately for the best result.**

Serves 4 • Preparation 20 minutes • Cooking 20 minutes

Tarte Tatin Cake

2 tablespoons margarine
¼ cup brown sugar
1 large pear, peeled, quartered and sliced into wedges
2 eggs
⅓ cup sugar
75g/2½ oz Lola's bread and pastry flour (page 7)
2 teaspoons gluten-free baking powder

Dairy-Free Custard
¼ cup sugar
2 Lola's sauce blocks (page 9)
1 egg, beaten
2 teaspoons vanilla extract

1 Preheat the oven to 360°F/180°C. Liberally grease a 8 in/20cm cake pan, using all the margarine. Sprinkle the brown sugar over the margarine. Overlap the pear slices in the pan in a circular pattern.

2 Whisk the eggs and sugar until creamy, add the flour and baking powder, and pour over the pears. Bake for 25 minutes. Invert the cake onto a flat plate and serve with custard.

3 To make the custard, bring one cup of water and ¼ cup sugar to a boil. Add two sauce blocks and let stand until softened. Return to low heat and whisk until the mixture thickens. Add the beaten egg and vanilla. Stir gently over low heat for 1 minute. Do not let boil.

Traditionally made with apples, this new twist uses pears and a simple batter for an easy and impressive dessert. The fruit gets caramelized and juicy and pairs well with the rich vanilla custard.

Serves 4 • Preparation 25 minutes • Cooking 30 minutes

Apple Cobbler

4 large baking apples, such as Jonathan, Braeburn, Gala or Granny Smith
100g/3½ oz sugar
1 tablespoon butter
1 large egg
100g/3½ oz Lola's bread and pastry flour (page 7)
60g/2 oz sugar
1 teaspoon gluten-free baking powder

1 Preheat the oven to 360°F/180°C. Cook the apples, 100g/3½ oz of sugar, and ¼ cup of cold water until soft. Pour into a greased 8 in/20cm baking dish.

2 Add the butter to ¼ cup of hot water. Set aside. In a large bowl, beat the egg and 2 oz/60g of sugar together until thick and creamy. Stir in the flour and baking powder, then the cooled water and butter mixture.

3 Pour the batter over apples and bake until golden, 10–15 minutes. Serve warm with whipped cream or ice cream.

Serves 4 • Preparation 25 minutes • Cooking 15 minutes

Cheesecake

Base
60g/2 oz butter
1 tablespoon honey
125g/4 oz crushed wheat-free biscuit crumbs or gluten-free corn cereal
45g/1½ oz shredded coconut

Filling
500g/16 oz cream cheese
250g/8 oz ricotta cheese
1 tablespoon sour cream
200g/7 oz sugar
2 eggs
2 tablespoons vanilla extract
dash of nutmeg

Topping
1 cup whipped cream
grated chocolate

1 Preheat oven to 300°F/150°C.
2 To make the crust, melt the butter and honey over a low heat and mix with the cereal or crumbs. You may need a little hot water if the cereal is dry. Combine with the coconut and press into a springform pan.
3 To make the filling, beat the cheeses and sour cream with the sugar until creamy. Add the eggs one at a time and whip on high speed. Stir in the vanilla and pour the mixture into the uncooked crust. Sprinkle with nutmeg and bake in the center of the oven for 1 hour. Turn the heat off and leave in the oven for and additional hour to set.
4 Chill before serving. Garnish with whipped cream and shaved chocolate.

Serves 4 • Preparation 35 minutes • Cooking 1 hour

Peach Strudel

4 large peaches, peeled and sliced
1 tablespoon gelatin
100g/3½ oz butter
1 egg yolk, white reserved
300g/10 oz Lola's all-purpose flour (page 7)
¾ cup sugar
2 tablespoons confectioner's sugar, for dusting

1 Preheat the oven to 360°F/180°C. Soak the gelatin in ¼ cup cold water, then heat gently until dissolved. Cool.
2 Combine butter, egg yolk, flour with the gelatin mixture in a food processor and process to form a firm pastry.
3 Press half of the dough into an ungreased 8 in/20cm square pan to form bottom crust. Arrange the sliced peaches and sprinkle with ½ cup sugar.
4 Roll out the other half of the pastry for the top of the strudel. Cut pastry into strips and use to form a lattice over the fresh peach slices.
5 Glaze with the reserved egg white and sprinkle with remaining ¼ cup sugar. Place in the oven and bake for 35 minutes. Dust with confectioner's sugar.

To peel peaches, make an X in the bottom of each peach with a sharp knife. Drop into boiling water for one minutes, then place in ice water for another minute. The skins will slip right off.

Serves 4 • Preparation 40 minutes • Cooking 35 minutes

Sponge Cake

2 eggs
75g/2½ oz sugar
75g/2½ oz Lola's all-purpose flour (page 7)
2 teaspoon gluten-free baking powder
2 teaspoons margarine

1 Preheat the oven to 360°F/180°C. Grease and flour an 8 in/20cm tart pan or flan cake pan.

2 Whisk the eggs and sugar over hot water until they are just warm and bubbly. Using an electric beater, beat until the mixture is thick and creamy but not stiff. Fold the flour and baking powder into the egg mixture.

3 Melt the margarine in 2 tablespoons of boiling water and pour down the inside of the bowl containing the batter. Turn the mixture with a wire whisk, being careful not to over-mix as this will release the air and flatten the sponge.

4 Pour into the pan and gently move the mixture with a spatula so that a small depression is made in the center of the cake. Place in the center of the oven and bake for 15 minutes. Let cool for 5 minutes before removing from the pan.

This is a great base for many desserts—make it ahead and freeze until ready to serve, topped with fresh berries, plums, peaches, or a simple dusting of powdered sugar. It's also used for the berry gateau on page 183.

Serves 2–4 • Preparation 30 minutes • Cooking 20 minutes

Berry Gâteau

1 sponge cake (page 180)
250g/8 oz strawberries
100g/3½ oz blueberries
100g/3½ oz sugar
100g/3½ oz raspberry jam
2 egg whites
200g/7 oz powdered sugar

1 Preheat oven to 400°F/200°C. Cut cooled cake into thirds, lengthwise. Set aside three strawberries for decorating the top of the cake.

2 Slice the remaining strawberries and cook on medium low heat with blueberries and sugar until soft and syrupy. In a separate pan, gently warm the raspberry jam until smooth.

3 On a large serving plate, arrange bottom layer of cake, spread with half of the berry mixture. Top with another layer of cake, and rest of berry mixture. Top with the final layer of cake and spread with melted jam.

4 Beat egg whites and powdered sugar on high speed until mixture is shiny and stiff peaks form. Starting on the top, frost the cake with meringue, carefully pulling the meringue down the sides of the cake to cover.

5 Bake for 15 minutes and top with reserved berries dipped in jam.

Serves 4–6 • Preparation 35 minutes • Cooking 15 minutes

Lemon Pudding

2 tablespoons margarine
200g/7 oz sugar
zest and juice of 2 lemons
4 eggs, separated
3 tablespoons Lola's bread and pastry flour (page 7)
1 cup milk

1 Preheat the oven to 360°F/180°C. Grease an ovenproof baking dish or four ramekins with margarine. Cream together the margarine, sugar, zest and egg yolks.

2 Add the sifted flours, milk and juice – stir to combine. Separately beat the egg whites until stiff and fold into the mixture.

3 Pour into the baking dish or ramekins and bake in the center of the oven for 20–25 minutes, until firm to the touch, but still a little wobbly. Serve warm with ice cream.

4 Cook for approximately 20–25 minutes until the sponge is firm to touch. As there is custard underneath the sponge, the pudding will be a little wobbly when it is cooked. Serve warm with cream or ice cream.

Serves 4 • Preparation 20 minutes • Cooking 25 minutes

Anzacs

60g/2 oz rolled rice flakes
¼ cup olive oil
200g/7 oz sugar
1 tablespoon honey
1 tablespoon light corn syrup
150g/5 oz Lola's all-purpose flour (page 7)
1 tablespoon pumpkin pie spice
100g/3½ oz shredded coconut
1 teaspoon baking soda

1 Preheat the oven to 340°F/170°C. Line one or two baking sheets with parchment paper. Place the rolled rice flakes in a saucepan and pour ½ cup of boiling water over them. Simmer for five minutes.

2 Add the oil, sugar, honey, and corn syrup to a medium-sized saucepan and warm gently for a few minutes (for a crisper cookie, bring to a boil). Stir in the warm rice flakes, then add the flour, spice and coconut. Finally, add the baking soda dissolved in 1 tablespoon of boiling water and mix this stiff mixture well.

3 Spoon onto the parchment sheets allowing room to spread and press down. Bake for 15 minutes and cool on the trays. For a less crisp result, reduce the oven temperature to 300°F/150°C. Store in an airtight container.

Serves 4 • Preparation 25 minutes • Cooking 15 minutes

Strawberry Shortcake

4 eggs
100g/3½ oz sugar
2 teaspoons margarine
1 tablespoon glycerine
100g/3½ oz Lola's bread and pastry flour (page 7)
2 teaspoons gluten-free baking powder
2 teaspoons vanilla extract
powdered sugar for dusting

Filling
150g/5 oz fresh strawberries
1 cup whipped cream

1 Preheat the oven to 360°F/180°C. Grease the sides and line the bottom of two 8 in/20cm round cake pans with parchment paper. Place the eggs and sugar in a large metal bowl and hand whisk over a saucepan of hot water until the mixture is slightly warm and frothy.

2 Remove from the heat and continue beating with a rotary or electric mixer until the mixture is thick and creamy but not stiff. Add the margarine and glycerine to 4 tablespoons of hot water and let stand for 1 minute.

3 Fold in the sifted flours and baking powder to the beaten eggs and powdered sugar. Mix in the vanilla extract, glycerine mix. Fold lightly but thoroughly.

4 Pour into the prepared pans, level with a spatula, and cook for 30 minutes. Let cool in the pan for 1 minute before turning out onto a wire rack to cool.

5 Set aside 8 small strawberries for decorating the top of the shortcake. Slice remaining strawberries and gently fold into the whipped cream. Spread ⅔ of the whipped cream mixture between the two cakes. Decorate the top with remaining whipped cream and reserved berries. Plate and dust with powdered sugar.

Serves 2–4 • Preparation 45 minutes • Cooking 30 minutes

Index